# Why Kids Can't Spell

## *A Practical Guide to the Missing Component in Language Proficiency*

ROBERTA HEEMBROCK

Rowman & Littlefield Education
*Lanham • New York • Toronto • Plymouth, UK*

Published in the United States of America
by Rowman & Littlefield Education
A Division of Rowman & Littlefield Publishers, Inc.
A wholly owned subsidary of The Rowman & Littlefield Publishing Group, Inc.
4501 Forbes Boulevard, Suite 200, Lanham, Maryland 20706
www.rowmaneducation.com

Estover Road
Plymouth PL6 7PY
United Kingdom

British Library Cataloguing in Publication Information Available

**Library of Congress Cataloging-in-Publication Data**

Heembrock, Roberta, 1959–
  Why kids can't spell : a practical guide to the missing component in language
proficiency / Roberta Heembrock.
    p. cm.
  Includes bibliographical references.
  ISBN-13: 978-1-57886-844-5 (cloth : alk. paper)
  ISBN-10: 1-57886-844-0 (cloth : alk. paper)
  ISBN-13: 978-1-57886-845-2 (pbk. : alk. paper)
  ISBN-10: 1-57886-845-9 (pbk. : alk. paper)
  eISBN-10: 1-57886-898-X
  eISBN-13: 978-1-57886-898-8
  1. English language—Orthography and spelling—Study and teaching
(Elementary)—Juvenile literature. 2. English language—Orthography and spelling—
Study and teaching (Middle school)—Juvenile literature. I. Title.
  LB1574.H44 2008
  372.63'2—dc22                                                    2008013951

♾ ™ The paper used in this publication meets the minimum requirements of
American National Standard for Information Sciences—Permanence of
Paper for Printed Library Materials, ANSI/NISO Z39.48-1992.
Manufactured in the United States of America.

In memory of Mom who always said,
"You can do anything you put your mind to!"

# Contents

# Acknowledgments

This book is a collective endeavor through the help, advice and encouragement of many people. My sincere gratitude and huge hugs to the following: The encouraging, inquisitive and conscientious Thomas F. Koerner, Ph.D., Vice President and Editorial Director of Rowman & Littlefield Education. Thanks for your belief and continuous support.

The awe-inspiring and talented Lynda Phung, assistant production editor, and Paul J. Cacciato, assistant managing editor of Rowman & Littlefield Education. You both kept me looking forward and constantly thinking.

David Doake, Ph.D., retired professor of education, at Acadia University. A truly wonderful and passionate educator and who is missed dearly.

Shane Templeton, Ph.D., foundation professor of literacy studies at the University of Nevada, Reno and J. Richard Gentry, Ph.D., author of *Breakthrough in Beginning Reading and Writing* and Jo Phenix, author of *The Spelling Teacher's Handbook* and *Spelling for Parents*, who all dedicated their time and expertise in the research for this book.

The fabulous group of reader reviewers, who unselfishly give their time to read, critique and supply their comments for the original manuscript, you all were terrific.

Kudos to all the students and your terrific work. This book is a result of your fabulous work. Keep on writing!

My friends and family, who encouraged me, supported me and kept me on task, especially, Sara and Natalie Heembrock, Barb Mac Beath,

Andrea Heembrock, Narmin Ismail-Teja, Kate Newburn, Peggy Squire, and Nancy Irvine.

My big sister, Louise, my lifetime mentor, thanks for all your reading, editing, encouragement and enthusiasm.

And especially, my loving husband, Peter, the techie, collector, editor, and organizer of this book. Your help and support have been amazing and very much appreciated. Thanks too for taking care of the kids and for being so patient with, "I just have one more thing."

# Foreword

It is rare indeed when a book such as *Why Kids Can't Spell: A Practical Guide to the Missing Component in Language Proficiency* is offered for parents and teachers. Written with the knowledge of an educator and the love of a parent, this book is a wonderfully crafted resource that does so much more than help parents and teachers help children learn to spell. Yes, our children are growing up in an age of digital technology with word processing spellcheckers. Roberta Heembrock demonstrates how spelling knowledge remains critically important, however, for writing and for reading. No software program can cuddle like a parent when reading a favorite book to a child or gently guide the child in sounding out the spelling of a word in a letter to grandma. Roberta provides parents all they need to know for building the larger context for learning to spell and for setting up a literate environment at home. She provides teachers solid recommendations for establishing a similar environment in the classroom.

Spelling involves so much more than simply getting down the right letters in the correct sequence, and learning how to spell is not merely a process of rote memorization. Roberta guides us through an understanding of how the spelling system of English really works. True, although we don't spell most words "the way they sound" in English, this is not necessarily a bad thing at all. You will learn why this is so and, in turn, learn how to guide children's developing understanding of spelling as a supportive and exciting process of discovery.

Roberta has structured each chapter in this book as only a gifted teacher could do. She shares with you what is to be learned, and then engagingly walks you through how to teach it. Through delightful examples from children's writing, she helps you learn that a child's understanding of spelling—in a larger sense, of how words work—is a developmental process. She explains and walks you through a wealth of strategies and activities to guide your child's development. Because spelling is not an isolated skill but exists in the context of reading, writing, talking, and listening, she offers strategies and skills that support your child's growth and development in all of these areas.

You are in for some surprises as well: What begins in your child's writing as random marks and later becomes quite strange and unusual spellings, actually reveals a wondrous and impressive logic. Roberta will help you understand this logic underlying your young child's attempts to spell words and how you may respond to and facilitate those attempts. And as your child grows and learns—or if your child is already older and you are wondering what to do—you may be surprised to learn how you can help him or her learn that the way we spell words offers powerful clues about their meaning. This is where learning about spelling and learning about vocabulary become closely connected. If you are a classroom teacher, this spelling/vocabulary connection will provide fascinating and compelling instructional opportunities.

If it has not become apparent already, I would like to emphasize that you and your child (or children!) are in for a marvelous, instructive, and enjoyable journey. In reading this book, I have learned much; I know you will as well!

Shane Templeton, Ph.D.
Foundation Professor of Literacy Studies
University of Nevada, Reno

# Introduction
## HOW THIS BOOK WORKS

Success is a journey—not a destination.

—Arthur Robert Ashe Jr., Famous
African American world class tennis star

Humans are social interacting beings. Since the time that man gathered in groups, we have strived to provide a way of communicating and permanently preserving our thoughts, beliefs, and ideas. It is very much a basic human need. Written language, a symbol of our beliefs, thoughts, and ideas, has become a vehicle for communication within our societal structure. The effectiveness of written communication directly relates to how well one can express oneself on paper. Thus, our society highly values the art of writing.

Furthermore, the way we write and the vocabulary we use is often a measure of our intellectual, educational, and social status. Likewise, standardized written language can provide greater stability and effectiveness when conveying our meaning. Mistakes can confuse the reader and discourage him or her from reading on. Improper spelling can even result in an incorrect or misleading message. Correct spelling is therefore critical to communication.

What is the most effective way to teach spelling? How does a learner learn to spell? What are the best methods to study spelling? Good questions! There does not seem to be a "textbook" or "recipe card" answer. However, research has shown that the understanding of the spelling process has been greatly oversimplified. It is indeed more than merely memorizing a list of words and reproducing them on paper. Spelling is a developmental and complex problem-solving process where spoken language becomes written language. There is substantial research supporting the idea that learning and teaching strategies for spelling should follow some basic guidelines and principles:

1. Spelling is learned through experimentation with language. We learn to read and write in a similar way as to how we learn to speak. Infants speak a language of their own which is an attempt at or an imitation of language. Often, it is only the mom or dad who can understand the child. As the child grows and is immersed in spoken language, his or her usage becomes more intelligible and complex. According to research, the best way to gain experience with written language is through purposeful connections between reading, writing, and spelling. Skills and strategies should be taught within the context of the child's personal reading and writing, at his or her level.

2. The spelling process is a problem solving activity that fosters independence and responsibility. A child's writing confidence and spelling development is enhanced when they are allowed to make mistakes, risk ideas and spelling attempts, and become editors of his or her own work.

3. Spelling errors are vitally important to the writing process. They tell the story. They tell what is known and what is still needed to learn. Spelling errors are the building blocks to the creation of a solid understanding of language conventions.

4. Develop a spelling "conscience" and "correctness."

5. Spelling needs to be taught in a safe, nonthreatening environment. Encourage risk-taking that does not impede student writing. Research has shown those students who had positive experience with their writing are the risk-takers and are more willing to attempt new style and ideas. Children who receive negative feedback about their writing, with constant remarks about this word and that word not spelled correctly, and that "when I was your age, I could . . . " and so on, are less willing to write and often become discouraged and uninterested in writing. Children at younger ages are writing more complex stories with complicated plots, characters, and dialogue, and are attempting more styles and so forth than ever before.

6. The family is fundamentally important in a child's reading, writing, and spelling development. They are the facilitators and role models. Be willing, informed, and prepared to accept the challenge and thrill of working with your child in this exciting endeavor.

*Why Kids Can't Spell: A Practical Guide to the Missing Component in Language Proficiency* is a spelling resource reference book. It is written for parents and educators who have an interest in and a concern for the teaching of correct spelling. The purpose of this book is to encourage and foster good spelling practices in the home, while reflecting today's teaching methods.

The design of this book is constructed in a scope and sequence format in which each chapter builds on the previous one. Every chapter includes a discussion on spelling background knowledge. This section focuses on an examination and analysis of children's writing samples, relating to J. Richard Gentry's Model of Spelling Development (Gentry 1987). This is followed by numerous inquiry-based, project-based generative ideas and activities.

The activities in this book are easy to prepare and understand, and use readily available materials. These activities are practical, meaningful, and effective. Remember that all chapters are related to each other, so choose to become familiar with all of them. Feel free to browse and borrow, and to adapt and modify the activities from any chapter in order to challenge and meet your own child's individual needs.

The back matter of this book is important and useful. Included are: the Appendix that includes J. Richard Gentry, Shane Templeton, and others' Model of Spelling Development, a comprehensive glossary of terms and definitions with examples, and a complete listing of references.

Inquiry-based, project-based, and generative teaching philosophy and methodology form the basis for this book. Gone is the belief that spelling should be an independent and isolated subject area. Experts in this field of study are encouraging a learning process where reading, writing, and spelling are not separate entities but one comprehensive activity.

I am here to say, "Go for it, have fun and enjoy the learning process!"

# CHAPTER 1

# Preschool Years

## Spelling Background Knowledge: Symbol to Print Concept

Look closely at each of the following children's attempts at writing. Carefully study each one and make some mental notes. What do these writing samples tell us? Do you notice any similarities to standard print? Are these children experiencing difficulty; are they writing at an independent level, at a frustration level?

Many parents have approached me for advice during parent interviews and meetings. Mostly, they want to know what an average child's writing normally looks like. They want to know if their child is average, or below or above average. They also ask for advice on how they can help their child become a better writer and speller.

The writing samples presented here are typical preschool writings. Each child's writing sample is very different and yet quite similar. Neither sample is right nor wrong nor more correct than the other. They are mere representations of each child's writing at this particular point in time.

Glen's sample is characteristic of an emergent writer (see figure 1.1). He has included pictures and loopy, wavy, and pointed lines to tell his story about rabbits. He has also included various circles, and upward and downward strokes. Glen has written continuously without the use of spacing. Additionally, his writing is spread all over the page without any perceivable rhyme or reason. Glen has tried to include both upper- and lowercase

1

**Figure 1.1.    Glen's writing sample**

letters in his writing, although seemingly indiscriminately. Note that his use of uppercase letters is incorrect. Notice also that Glen has written the uppercase letter *N* backwards. These are not uncommon mistakes. Furthermore, it is not uncommon either to encounter children who reproduce letters upside down or even as complete mirror images of the standard letter.

Krista's sample is also representative of a young writer (see figure 1.2). She continues to use wavy, loopy, and pointed lines and circles to express her story about Indians. If you look closely, you can also see that she has tried to reproduce some letters. Krista seems to have progressed beyond picture-like to more print-like writing. She has become more adept at making more standard representations of letters. Her work still appears to be haphazard, randomly selected, and composed. Furthermore, it seems as though she writes without left-to-right knowledge of print.

At first glance, it is difficult to view these "scribbles" as actual written stories. Many people have considered children's scribbles at this age and experience to be just what they are. As one can clearly see though, this cannot be further from the truth. All the children here have incorporated, in their own unique way, specific characteristics of conventional print. These markings are

**Figure 1.2.    Krista's writing sample**

a child's writing. They are as important to the child's development in writing as babbling is to a baby's speech development and learning process.

Preschool children spend much time and effort experimenting. They explore with symbols, pictures, numbers, and letters in an attempt to reproduce written language. They understand that people compose information on paper and often attempt to imitate a person they observe writing. They understand that conventional writing contains various multiple marks and that those same marks make different spellings—only the order of the marks changes, not their existence. What they do not understand or perceive is the notion of "word." Children at first view their printed representations as a picture copy of their thoughts rather than written words. They believe that words need to look like the things they represent. They later learn to accept that words look different from their meanings and that specific sounds are associated with certain letters.

# Reading Ideas and Activities

### READ ALOUD

The single most important reading activity you can do, with a child of any age is reading aloud with them. Reading stirs the child's curiosity and introduces him to the world of imagination. It increases his general knowledge of the world and encourages him to explore and discover the unknown. Read, read, read, and then read some more.

**Figure 1.3.    Aunt Donnie and the cousins**

## SHARED READING

Shared reading is exactly what it sounds like—an interactive time when a story is read, shared, and collaboratively enjoyed by more than one person. It is a time for sharing, reading, laughing, and crying together! This can be carried out by simply encouraging echo reading (students repeating the words after the reader), choral reading (everyone reading at the same time together), or fill in-in-the-blank reading (the reader reading most of the text, only pausing when students are expected to fill in the blank—done mostly with rhyming words or other predictable words in the story).

These shared reading strategies are excellent activities to do with Big Books (oversized books with enlarged print and illustrations), and as the reader reads the book aloud, all of the audience members can see and appreciate the print and illustrations, even Grandpa.

## BOOK SELECTION

Selecting good reading material is difficult for the inexperienced. People are often unaware of what's out on the market. They wonder who the popular writers are. They want to know what an appropriate reading level is.

First and foremost, you must become an active participant in book knowledge. Familiarize yourself with popular authors and illustrators. Your neighborhood school, public librarian, or favorite bookstore clerk can direct you to some very good writers.

Consider a visit to your local bookstore. They often feature authors who attend book signings and book talks. Keep your eyes and ears open. These kinds of events are great, interesting, and very informative, so if possible do not miss an opportunity to attend one. Your local school also often has writers and illustrators attend the school as part of the library program. Once again, such an event would be worth your attendance and participation.

Another good source for recommended reading of new and old favorites is the book review section of your local newspaper. There are also many recommended reading lists available in print and on the Internet.

To gain further knowledge in children's literature, visit children's literature websites and discussion rooms. There are so many sites to visit and experience. Don't forget to check the reference section at the end of articles for the author's reading selection recomemndation.

Ask other parents, teachers, and librarians for recommendations. Look for books that have won children's literary awards and medals. When searching for good Big Books, always check first to see if they are also printed in regular book form. If they are, chances are they are already successful children's stories. This is a great tip that I have learned from my local librarian.

Here are some questions to consider when researching for good books:

- Is the subject matter right for my child's age?
- Is the book well made, strong enough to withstand my child's handling?
- Am I comfortable with what the book says or shows?
- Does it portray the lifestyles and values I agree with? What does it say about male and female roles and issues?
- Do I like the underlying philosophy of the book—what is it really saying?
- In the case of very young children, you also want to consider the following questions: Is the language repetitive and predictable? Are the pictures colorful and detailed? Are the events predictable?

When selecting books; make sure to choose a wide variety of genres, topics, authors, style, and so on. Children's magazines, concept books, ABC, and counting books are good sources of information. Fiction books, such as fairy tales and folk tales, are excellent pleasure reading books, as are mysteries, nursery rhymes and songs, and science fiction. Nonfiction books, such as biographies, travel books, or books about animals, are absolutely wonderful. It is fun to include different types of books in your personal library. Interactive books, such as the peek-a-boo books, palm books, and sound and talking books, are very popular with young children. Pop-up, push and pull, squeeze me, and touch and feel books are equally popular. Exposing children to a wide variety of reading material gives them the opportunity of finding out which books they are most interested in.

Look for books with suitable vocabulary that is at an appropriate level for your child. It is beneficial to keep in mind that reading and listening levels differ with readers. A person can more easily listen to than read a difficult and challenging book. Truthfully, choosing a higher reading level book for reading aloud with your child can encourage him to expand his horizons. He may eventually want to read the more challenging books in his own independent reading time. You may also look for books that present real vocabulary and use everyday language as we hear it spoken and see it in print on a daily basis. Choose books that use interesting and fun language.

Select books that have a good story. Look for books with interesting characters and settings. Find stories that have characters similar to your child's own age. Choose stories where the character has similar parallel life experiences as your child. Seek books with solid story structures and plots, books where the end of the story resolves story problems. Make certain the stories depict the ideas and morals that complement your lifestyle. Remember to look for their learning and creative thinking potential, books that inspire and motivate children.

It is important that the books you choose have good illustrations that comprise large, brilliantly colored and finely detailed drawings in various modern day mediums, such as water colors, paper art, sculptures, and even clay. Photography and pen and ink drawings continue to be classic mediums.

Most importantly, choose books that are fun for you to read and fun for your children to listen to. You can therefore include some of the favorite books of your childhood. Chances are that your children might enjoy them, too.

When selecting books for the very young, Picture Books, (books with little or no print) are wonderful. They teach story sequence and structure to emergent readers. The benefit of this type of book is that the storyteller can change his story every time he reads, while maintaining the picture meaning. Good picture books have large and beautiful illustrations that are meant to entice and elicit interest in children.

Another style of book to use with young children is the Big Book. These books are fun, colorful, and large. Children love them and can easily become immersed in them, as they are large as life. The large print is not only fun, it allows you to draw the child's attention to print and helps them to follow along while you are reading. It gives them opportunities to build connections between spoken language and print. You can find these books in most libraries, which have them, available on loan.

Good books for beginning readers include books with simple vocabulary, short sentences, and predictable and repetitive language. Recommended books should have large type and bold pictures and the language should be interesting and natural. The book itself should have sturdy and durable pages and bindings.

For shared-reading book selection, I cannot stress enough the importance of predictable books. Children remember text through repetitive, rhyming, and patterned language. They remember passages through picture clues and repetitive story sequences and structure. Children love to participate actively in the reading process and to retell these stories. Predictable books allow for these types of activities and give all children successful cues to help them read, while helping them develop early reading strategies, listening skills, and thinking skills.

## A LANGUAGE-RICH ENVIRONMENT

Once you have a good selection of reading material, the rest is easy. Children need to see the beauty, wonder, and delight that the written word creates. Help them by immersing them in a language-rich environment filled with stories.

*Econo-saver:* Buy secondhand books from store sales, garage sales, and flea markets. Think about swapping books with a friend or borrowing from your local library.

*Econo-saver:* Enroll your child in book clubs from his school. They are very reasonable in price. In Canada, one finds Elf for preschoolers and See-Saw for E.C.S. and Grade One children. Grades Two and Three children can enjoy Lucky; for Grades Four, Five, and Six, there is Arrow, and for students of Grade Seven, Eight, and Nine there is Tab.

*Econo-saver:* Buy your children magazine subscriptions. *Electric Company*, *Chickadee*, *Owl*, *Ranger Rick*, and *Stone Soup* are just some of the children's magazines on the market today.

One helpful suggestion is to place bookshelves in your child's reading room and fill them with books. A beanbag, an over-sized chair, large pillows, and a rocking chair are excellent additions. How about an old bathtub filled with pillows? Display as many books as you can at eye level with the covers facing outward.

*Econo-saver:* If you, a relative, or friend are handy with woodwork, build special bookracks. Design the bookracks like the card shelves in a card shop. These specially made racks hold dozens of books that face outward and make for easy selection.

*Econo-saver:* Keep your eyes open at auctions where these card racks may be available for auctioning. Watch for card stores going out of business. They often have them for sale.

It is important to make sure that there is ample and proper lighting in the reading room. Surround the room with props, posters, and pictures related to the books in the child's collection. You can also have on hand tapes and a tape recorder for talking books, and storybook CDs and a CD player (with a set of earphones to help you keep your sanity)! These room additions and changes encourage further reading skills. They reinforce the idea that reading is fun and enjoyable. They also give the child the expectation and permission to read at home.

A colleague of mine had a family room down in the basement dedicated to reading and books for her grandkids. The area contained an incredible number of books, the covers of which were clearly displayed facing outward in wall-to-wall bookcases.

In addition, other walls were studded with life-sized copies of storybook characters constructed from simple paper cutouts. What made them beautiful and inviting were their real-life costumes. Each story character had costumes made out of old scraps of material and jewelry. Bunches of "puffed-up" crinoline stuffed under the material adorned the story characters' dresses. Fake fur material was used as a lion's mane, and so on.

Every time I went to visit, I became intrigued and fascinated by the room. I often thought to myself, what a wonderful world of make-believe these lucky grandkids have.

It is important to set a standard reading time that is the same each day. Choose a time that suits your family's schedule, a time when you feel most relaxed and alert, and a time when you are less likely to be interrupted by the phone, television, or neighbors. Your goal is to determine a regular and committed time. Ultimately, you want the shared reading time to become a healthy habit. A time to spend a special moment with the ones you love. You and your child deserve to have fifteen to twenty minutes a day to spend together reading. Don't ever compromise!

Some popular reading times are: before bedtime or nap, immediately following supper or after playschool/school. How about reading together as a family on weekend mornings or afternoons? Reading together while taking a bath is also an excellent time. Think about taking a book with you to the doctor or dentist's office and spend the waiting time reading together.

Reading is a social sharing time among reader, author and listener. So, snuggle up, get cozy, and enjoy. Younger children love to sit in your lap, while older children love to snuggle up to you during a reading session. It is good to encourage and invite other siblings, friends, and relatives to read with your child. This gives you a break and allows the child to hear others read. It definitely gives the message that reading is for everyone.

Reading is a time for narrating those favorite stories in a supportive and nurturing environment. Do not concern yourself with teaching the mechanics and drill of reading. Keep in mind that your purpose at this level is to promote a lifelong love for reading. Prepare to talk, laugh, cry, and discuss your reading.

When reading with your child, use exciting and dramatic voices. Change your voice as the character or action changes. Use an exaggerated, yet compatible character voice. It feels awkward at first, but as your child responds enthusiastically, you'll become more comfortable and at ease. Listening to a person read a story increases one's knowledge of oral reading, specifically fluency, articulation, and voice intonation.

In the case of young children, keep the shared reading times brief and frequent. Discuss the pictures with the child to draw out what is happening in the story. Point to different objects, subjects, and scenes and label them for the child. Ask the child to name and label familiar things and have him tell what's happening in the pictures. Allow the child to talk about what he sees and his interpretation of the story, and relate events and characters to the child's own personal life and experiences. These kinds of activities help create picture association with language and the real world, as well as to develop comprehension.

## BOOK DISCUSSION

It is essential to discuss a book while reading together. Not only does it help to formulate reading patterns, standards, and comprehension, but it allows your child to become an active and constructive participant.

I, as a teacher, have always felt weak in this area though have understood its importance. I have worked very hard on this technique for many years. It feels awkward and contrived at first, but with practice it becomes natural.

I found out that it is good to ask open-ended questions, ones that elicit more than "yes," "no," or other single-word statements. As a rule of thumb, ask questions that begin with who, what, when, where, why, and how. Ask questions such as: What do you think this story is about? Why do you think the author chose to write about this topic? What do you think will happen in the story next? Who is telling the story? If you were to tell the story, in your own words, whose voice would you chose to tell it from and why? Where does the story take place? How do you think the story will end? If you could change the ending, what might you have happen? What was it that made you like or dislike this story? How did the story make you feel and why? Who was your favorite character and why? Were you reminded of anything in your own life? What new words did you learn?

Before you even open a book to begin to read the story, have your child take a look at the picture, title, and teaser (found on the backside of the book). Have him make predictions and guesses about the story. What clues are the author and book-cover designer giving us? Do you think the story is going to be happy, funny, or scary? Do you think it is real or make-believe? What do you know about the characters? Where is this story taking place? And so on. Spend lots of time gathering information and clues about the story. This helps your child to comprehend the story, gives him confidence with predicting events within the story, and helps him to be successful a reader in the future. Only then, move onto reading it together.

Whenever you are reading with your young child, be sure you track the words with your finger, always in a smooth and fluent fashion. Be careful not to interrupt the flow of reading with the tracking of the words. Finger tracking gives him certain reading knowledge. He learns that a book reads from beginning to end, left to right, and top to bottom. He also learns that there is a right side up and an upside down position.

For very young readers "pretend read" is a very critical step in the beginning-to-read process. Many children, as they repeatedly hear a passage, become secure and very familiar with the material and have essentially "memorized" the book. They are able to read the story, word for word, sentence by sentence. Many even adopt and use the same voice intonations and expressions as you used. All the children believe they are reading.

These beginning readers receive a great sense of satisfaction and accomplishment in this activity. Do not discredit their newfound confidence by saying they are not reading. Allow your emergent reader the opportunity to "pretend read." Compare a beginner's reading attempts to those from when the child was learning to speak or walk. After learning from memory, children begin to understand the connection between oral and written words.

During the shared reading process, it is beneficial to give a slight pause while you are waiting to encourage your child's participation. Give him a positive nod, clap, or statement to acknowledge and praise his participation.

When reading with children, remember to be patient. Don't force your child to sit with you and read. You don't need to finish the book, page, or even the sentence. Simply stop if you or your child loses interest in a particular book. Let him select a new one. His interest in reading grows if you give him patience, time, and room. Have faith—it all comes full circle ultimately. I can remember becoming very upset with my little one because she would not sit with me and read. She was constantly on the go. Eventually, I succumbed to letting her play while I read. I figured that at least she could hear me read. I felt very guilty and very much a failure. I have since spoken with other mothers and have found out that I am not the only one experiencing this difficulty. Similarly to me, other moms have resorted to just sitting and reading a story while their child plays. I know my daughter loves stories and story times. She'll constantly bring us her favorite ones and pat our legs, which is our cue to pick her up and let her sit with us while we read the story.

You must prepare yourself to teach and show children how to handle books, magazines, and other reading material with care and respect. Keep in mind that the more practice they have, the better they become. Supply your child with bookmarkers. Reinforce all covers with packing tape and even have the covers of your favorite "keeper" books laminated if necessary.

*Econo-saver*: If you can't laminate the covers of your favorite books, a good substitute is clear Mac-tac, which can be bought at any department store. It is inexpensive and easy to use.

*Econo-saver*: It is easy to make your own bookmarkers out of old cards or hand-decorated heavy paper. This could become a craft idea for you and your child to indulge in on a rainy day.

## MODELING

Place yourself in a position to be your child's role model, by letting the child observe you reading. You provide your child with the foresight into the importance of reading. Let the child watch and learn from you. Oftentimes, your attitude toward reading becomes your child's best motivator to read. Surround yourself with books, magazines, newspapers, or any appropriate print material.

One of my favorite reading places is the bathroom. In this room in my house, you'll find the *National Geographic, Reader's Digest, MacLean's,* and *People* magazines. I have gone so far as to set up a magazine rack to hold all the current issues.

Let your child watch you and older siblings learn to read. Teach your children that we read for many reasons, such as for pleasure (fiction and nonfiction, according to our tastes), for information gathering purposes (newspaper, magazines, and textbooks, etc.), and for instruction ("how to" cook, sew, write, assemble, build, and so on).

## THE LIBRARY

Your local community library is an excellent place to find a variety of books both for your children and yourself. It is a fabulous and exciting place to venture to on a Saturday morning. You can find something for people of all ages, interests, and tastes. It is at your disposal to take advantage of. One great hint: library cards make great birthday, Christmas, or year-end gifts.

I can remember going to the bookmobile every Saturday morning as a child with my family. The bookmobile was a library in a bus that traveled from community to community. I always looked forward to it and remember coming home with a bunch of new books. I would spend the rest of the day looking at and reading my new books.

When at the library, allow your child the experience of selecting his own books. Guide him to the appropriate age and reading ability section. Let him choose his books from there.

Most libraries organize their books by age, reading level, and subject. Some libraries further code reading levels into easy reading and advanced reading categories. If you are unsure of the organization of the books at your library, talk to your librarian. She or he is more than willing to help you out.

While at the library, choose some books for yourself. Let your child see you use and browse the library. Elicit your child's cooperation to select additional books for him to read, as well as some books for shared reading. If you're unsure of what would constitute good selections, your librarian, again, is an excellent resource. The librarian has invaluable and up-to-date knowledge of children's stories and popular books. Take your time and browse around, too. Old favorites tend to be good reading material for children. There are many types, styles, and forms of books to choose from.

Many libraries provide excellent free children and family programs. They often have toddler and preschool story times, puppet plays, and rhyme times. These are wonderful opportunities for your youngster to listen to stories and become familiar with the librarian. Your library may also offer special programs, such as fun nights, film and video evenings, and theme nights. Additionally, it may hold local interest sessions, hands-on-science extravaganzas, and even mystery evenings. It is always a good idea to become familiar with your library, its programs, and resource people.

When you return home from your trip to the library, your child should have a special and safe place to store his borrowed books. This place should be a designated place that is separate from his personal library. As with any book, children must know how to care for and respect them properly.


## FUN AND GAMES

You can do many reading-related activities in the comfort of your own home. When planning and implementing these activities, remember to keep school and home two very separate and distinct places. The home is an excellent place for one-on-one interactive instruction. You should make the activities game-like yet challenging.

Being a new mother of a young family, I know about time constraints and the importance of using one's time wisely and efficiently. Reading should be done in some form every single day. Shared reading—reading aloud together—is a wonderful activity to engage in with your child. USSR (uninterrupted sustained silent reading) and DEAR (drop everything and read) are quick and fun activities. You can have regular and scheduled times for these activities or you can do them whenever time permits. For children who cannot read by themselves, it would be a great idea to record their favorite stories on tape to assist with quick and independent reading.

Early in my career, I was the district's Resource Teacher for a rural community. This meant that I had to travel to several schools weekly. I did not have a permanent classroom. Instead, I had aides and teachers to carryout my programs when I was not at a particular location.

This type of teaching made it hard for me to establish individual reading times for the children. As a compromise, I had classroom volunteers and parents tape-record stories for me. I color-coded the books and tapes with matching colored stickers. Students who could not read could select the right tape and book independently by matching the colored stickers. I used zip-lock bags of all different sizes to store the books and keep them together. I also used colored stickers for the play, stop, and rewind functions on the tape recorder. I also taught all the children to use the recorder, and they were all instructed to rewind the tape for the next person. You can do the same thing at home. Older siblings, grandparents, and other relatives can make tape recordings of certain books you have chosen to put on tape. The older children can then color-code each book and tape and place them in zip-lock bags. Finally, teach your child how to use the tape recorder independently. When you experience one of those very busy nights, simply have your child listen to a taped story.

It would be great to encourage those readers who are taping stories to use lots of expression and voice changes when reading. During our preparations for a Grade Three listening center activity, my team partner and I convinced our librarian, assistant principal, and principal to participate in creating a tape-recorded reading. The kids just loved it, and we had a blast making the tape. One of the exercises we had the children do as part of the listening center was to identify all the readers.

## FAMILY NIGHT ACTIVITIES

Planned family nights, when you make and play different reading games and activities, are always a wonderful idea. The family of one of my students used to have regular family nights, which were actually scheduled on the calendar for every Thursday evening, as I recall. Throughout the year, each family member was responsible for the activities, agenda, and for reading a story to the family. It's so much more fun to plan these evenings together as a family, rather than going to the movies, renting a video, or even just watching television. Choose activities that everyone can participate in, and don't forget the popcorn.

Making Big Books is an excellent family activity that can be easily done at home. Simply go to a photocopy store and ask the merchant to enlarge pictures from your favorite storybook onto white sheets of paper. If you are good at drawing, you can even make your own reproductions of the pictures.

The next step allows everyone to participate and become active members in Big Book making. Gather your crayons, markers and pencil crayons, select a page, and begin to color the pages—make this a joint activity with your child.

You then cut the pictures out and glue them onto large sheets of paper. Remember to leave enough space for the print.

Next, rewrite the story using large print, carefully in pencil at first, and then copy the text with a permanent marker. This may seem like an unnecessary extra step; just the same, I remember spending hours making my own only to have it ruined when I used marker first without planning with a pencil.

If you want to keep your Big Book and to allow your children to handle it, you may want to consider getting it laminated at the photocopy store. You can keep the pages separate or bind them with punched holes and rings. I would recommend keeping the pages loose. This way you can place them on the floor, spread them out, and crawl all around them with your child.

Your child can then memorize the story and recite it later at a planned family night. I did this with a special education class. I enlarged and traced the book's pictures and printed the text in large print. The students colored the pages and decided where the print should go—a great story sequencing project. The story was then memorized and rehearsed. When everyone was ready, we went to a retirement home and presented the story in a dramatic presentation. Each student had a page of the story draped around their neck and each student turned around and read his or her page in turn.

Big Book making really goes a long way toward building family ties and bridging the "generation gap." Furthermore, it builds self-esteem and reinforces the idea that reading is fun. There are several quick, educational, and fun activities you can do with your Big Book. You can do some word mystery close exercises. For this kind of activity, just place masking tape over the laminated words on different pages. Have your child search and hunt for the missing words, then ask him to find the missing word by telling you what the exact word the author used was. I would accept any logical or reasonable replacement word. You then write the word for him on the masking tape. Re-read what you've written and together enjoy the original story or your new and revised story. One suggestion would be to start by blanking out nouns first, followed by action words (verbs), and finally by descriptive words (adjectives). This is a good, "small-step" sequence.

You can easily plan some sequence and order exercises with the loose pages from your homemade Big Book. This can be done by mixing up the pictures from your Big Book and spreading them on the floor. Give your child the task of rearranging the pictures and placing them in proper sequential order according to the story. Remember to blank out the page numbers when you do this activity. Kids are smart and clue into the numbering system. To further challenge your child, you can complete the same using the written paragraphs.

There are also some basic arts and crafts ideas you can do with your child. Here are some examples:

- Cut out felt characters and scenes from your child's favorite story. Have him retell the story using a flannel board. Mix up the events from the story and have your child rearrange them in proper chronological order.
- Create puppets, as simple as paper bag characters or stuffed sock characters, all the way to the more elaborate papier-mâché characters. Create a puppet stage out of an old refrigerator box or an even more intricate one out of wood, hinges, and hooks. Role-play and act out the story.
- Another idea would be to enlist your child's help in building a diorama of your child's favorite scene. What you need for this activity is a shoebox and various types of drawing material. Other requirements are scissors, glue, crayons, and a great imagination. Have the child color the background scenes on the inner sides of the box. Then have her draw and cut out stand-up figures and objects and glue them inside the box, in front of the backdrop. The purpose is to retell the story, with your child, using the diorama.
- You can even make up a different ending than the original story. You can either draw the new ending or just act it out. It would do a lot to a child's imaginative powers to encourage him to produce a new story using the basic story structure and sequence. Most importantly, this would be a moment of sharing.

- How about baking some cookies or a Father's Day breakfast together with your child? Cooking requires one to read and interpret recipes.
- Another alternative could be to plan some activities for Sunday dinner following the family night routine. One Sunday evening, some friends had my family over for dinner. They had invited my entire family and another friend, Sharon, who is as close to us as a sister. She, too, is an elementary teacher. That evening, Sharon and I entertained the kids by reading from books the kids had brought with them. We shared the reading parts and had a terrific time acting out the stories. The kids' ages ranged from ten months to sixty-nine years. All the "kids" had a blast and asked us to re-read the stories several times. By the end of the evening, poor Sharon became exhausted after all of her antics. Oh my, what fun we had! The communication that is naturally inspired during reading times has such a way of developing family relationships, attitudes, and values.

You may adapt any of these suggestions or come up with your own ideas, don't forget to ask your child to provide his input. The idea is to create more family-bonding time. Make sure to include fun activities during family trips and outings on weekends and holidays. Something else to think about—plan a "book-nic," that is, pack up a lunch, a blanket and some books, and head to the nearest park, then read and eat to your hearts' content.

## Writing Ideas and Activities

Preschoolers learn about our spelling system through experimentation and discovery. As they become exposed to a print-enriched world, they also begin to understand and figure out the relationship between writing and speech. Children require time to explore and examine print. They need opportunities to try and copy writing. Children need to "test" the boundaries of writing by comparing their attempts with standard writing. It is the process of writing that is important, not the clarity of the writing itself.

From the time a child can hold a crayon, writing should become a part of their everyday life. Preschoolers are at an age where they are constantly asking "why." They can use and manipulate oral language. It is the perfect time to incorporate their "whys" into written and pictorial form. Introducing children to printed language is important. It helps to foster and continue their love of language, from a spoken language to a written one.

You, as a parent, have an important role to play. It is imperative that you become an active participant. Remember how you held his hands as he was learning to walk. You were an important part of those first few steps. You can also be an important part of his first steps in writing. Talk to him about writing. Take the time to explain, discover, and dream. Allow him to broaden his experience base in this manner.

## WRITING CENTER

When working with young eager writers, it is important to create a writing center in your home. This provides a place and time for writing and gives a young writer permission to write. The child sees that mom and dad consider writing a valued activity.

It is important that this center be seen as a safe and a personal haven. You then need to support your child's writing with constant praise and encouraging feedback. You must remember that a child's writing is never wrong, but rather a developmental process. It showcases the child's present level of writing knowledge and understanding. As they experiment with language, children's writing skills progress.

A writing center should have many sheets of paper for all kinds of writing. It is best to supply sheets of various colors, including the fluorescent ones. Paper of various shapes, such as squares, diamonds, and circles would be wonderful and fun. You can also think about holiday shapes, such as Christmas tree cutouts, Easter basket cutouts, and umbrella cutouts. Size is also important—palm size, regular size, legal size, and poster size paper are all found in stores. Try also to include various textures—newsprint, construction, onion, crepe, and tissue are only some examples of types of paper. Furthermore, you can include books of wallpaper samples and stationery in your child's writing center.

*Econo-saver*: Most newspaper companies give free blank newsprint paper to the public. Called "roll ends," they are literally the end rolls left over from printing. Just contact the Marketing Resource Department of your local newspaper office to find out if they have any available.

It is important to give your child mostly unlined paper to work with. Lined paper tends to create boundaries and can cause a child to become too concerned with staying within the lines. Consequently, the child's creative thoughts become stifled.

Also included in your writing center should be baskets of pens, pencils, and pencil crayons. One can find all kinds of wonderful writing utensils in stores today—anything from fabric pens to water-soluble markers to crayons to different kinds of paints. The writing implements should be both wide and fine-tipped.

*Econo-saver*: Rather than purchasing baskets to hold your child's writing utensils, you can use empty baby-wipe boxes. They are a perfect size for pens, pencils, and other writing utensils.

## WRITING TOOLS

When deciding on what writing tools to use, keep in mind the proper size. You can buy large-sized crayons, markers, and pencils. If you cannot find what you want, you can think about getting some pencil grips. These are made of plastic; they are formfitting and easily slide over a pencil.

Pencil grips are available in two styles. The Triangular Pencil Grip is a three-sided utensil. When placed on a pencil, a person can confidently grip the pencil with the first three fingers. The second one is a Streto Pencil Grip. It is gum-like and has three fingered imprints. These "grippers" make writing easier for small children and those with dexterity or fine-motor difficulties.

*Econo-saver*: If you are unable to buy a pencil grip, you can make your own. Simply wrap an elastic band around your writing instrument. Use as many elastic bands as you need to achieve a comfortable fit.

Why limit your writing tools to just ordinary pens and paper? Think variety. How about having your child use an old typewriter, the computer, or even stencils? Other great options would be letter stamps and inkpads, slates, and chalk. Magnetic writing slates with wooden pencils, acetate paper, and wipe-off cloths are particularly fun. Finger paints and soap-flake paints (search the Internet for recipes) also make writing a great and playful experience.

**Figure 1.4.   Matthew, Mom, and Thomas**

## SAFETY

Remember to include in your writing center a child-safe pair of scissors, glue, staples, stapler, and a hole punch. Erasers, a clipboard, ruler, and pencil sharpener also come in useful, as are paper clips, paper fasteners, sticky notes, and stickers. Basically, anything to aid in the writing process would be a welcome addition, as long as consideration is taken with respect to overzealous children and the probable eventuality of messy spills and accidents.

Child safety and comfort should be foremost in your mind. To ensure this, you must establish a definite set of boundaries, and identify them with clarity and precision. Physically show your child the writing center's location. Show him what he can and cannot do while he spends time in the center.

This is the time when you can work together to develop some commonly agreed basic rules, including setting consequences to misbehavior. It is best not to have too many rules; four or five points would suffice. The rules should not be too cumbersome, rather straightforward and simple.

Place the rules and consequences on a poster and display it in a prominent place in the writing center.

Remember to discuss and demonstrate clean-up expectations. To lessen undue stress and frustration, place a plastic table cloth on the table and a slab of old linoleum on the floor permanently in the writing center. It would help to also have lots of old newspapers at hand. You can hang up dad's old shirt or a waterproof apron to use for messy jobs, and make it readily available for the child to put on as the need arises.

If a child does a lot of drawing and writing, make sure to have proper lighting. Purchase a good reading lamp. Think about the use of natural day light when setting up a writing center. Proper lighting is so crucial for the maintenance of good healthy eyesight.

Your child's own bedroom is always a comfortable place for a writing center. If he has his own table and chair or desk, this environment encourages writing. Other places to consider are the basement, the recreation room, the kitchen, and family room. The writing center should be located in any area where your child feels comfortable. When these suggestions have been followed and a writing center is well in place, a child can work contentedly and free of worry.

A good friend of mine allowed her children to use the kitchen floor. She always kept a corner covered with taped white paper near a cupboard. In the cupboard were her children's paper, pencils, crayons, paints, and markers. The children were given permission to use that area freely. The only set rule was that they were responsible for cleaning up their mess afterwards.

If you cannot provide your child with a writing center area, you could try filling an old suitcase with writing material. Many teachers, whom I know, use a mobile suitcase to encourage writing at home. Inside this suitcase is writing material of all kinds for a child to take home and use. Once that child has finished with the suitcase, she then returns it to the school to be restocked for another student to use.

You can surely find an old suitcase, trunk, or plastic storage box at your home. Perhaps you could even decorate an old box and lid with durable, long-lasting material. You can then fill the suitcase with stationery items, including many of the items mentioned above for the writing center. Organize all the items into zip-lock bags and pencil cases.

Allow your child to use the suitcase on rainy days and Saturday mornings. Have her use the suitcase when she is sick or has nothing to do. You must remember to have your child restock the suitcase and clean up the mess afterwards.

My husband's family used something similar. They had an old toy box filled with writing paraphernalia and crafts. He remembers using and enjoying the box many times as a child. His favorite game was playing "office." Again, in my husband's household, the kids were responsible for cleaning up after themselves.

An important thing to remember is to find a place and time to display and honor your child's work. His work should be featured in some central place where he feels it is being acknowledged and valued. Good places for display would be the refrigerator, the family room, or even the bedroom walls.

Purchase a cheap cork bulletin board and place it on the family room wall at your child's eye level. Let him put his own work on "display," although sometimes you may suggest pieces to display. Another place to exhibit your child's writing is at the office. Children love to "show-off" their work and would be proud to have mom or dad value their work enough to display it at the office.

Have a favorite piece decorated and framed by the child using a painted cardboard cutout and different accent accessories (such as sequins, beads, shells, feathers, etc.). Buy a wooden frame from a craft store, choose a funky colored or textured spray paint, and paint the frame. You can even have the artwork professionally framed.

Another important thing to remember is to always have your child write his name and date on his work. He should be responsible for and take ownership of his work.

When the writing center is firmly in place and lots of materials are available, be sure to engage your child in many creative writing activities. Choose to make the activities fun-filled and family interactive. This helps to build a long-lasting, home-learning environment.


## MODELING

Along with modeling reading, modeling writing is so very important. You are their first role model. Take it with pride and complete enthusiasm. You can model writing by:

- Leaving little notes around the house for your children. Depending on their reading ability, the message can consist of wordless pictures, Rebus messages (the substitution of pictures in placement of hard words; for example, "I ♥ you"), or full-length written notes.

- Write morning messages, morning routines, and don't-forgets on a white board.
- Sneak warm-fuzzy notes in their backpacks or with their lunch snacks.
- Let them see you write a letter to Grandma and have them add to your letter.
- Allow them to observe you composing a grocery list. Let them add to the grocery list. We have a white board for listing food requests. Everyone is encouraged to write their requests down. Sometimes the board becomes a place for jokes and one-up-on-you statements. My daughters are learning French in school, and lately I've noticed the food requests written in French.

These kinds of activities are very beneficial. They illustrate the purpose and function of writing, increase a child's knowledge and understanding of writing, and demonstrate that writing is useful and meaningful.

## LETTER KNOWLEDGE

To encourage letter knowledge, teach your child alphabet rhymes, poems, and songs. Teach your child the Alphabet song. There is the American and Canadian version. Rehearse it many times until the child has learned it from memory. Together, make up a new personalized alphabet song using words from your child's environment. For example:

> A, B, C, D, E, F, G,
> I have a cat that lives in Calgary.
> H, I, J, K, L, M, N, O, P,
> She is as cute and smart as can be.

Make your own set of alphabet cards. Draw large stencil letters, in both upper- and lowercase print on heavy Bristol board. Help your child cut the cards into uniform sizes. Add magazine pictures or homemade pictures and a written label. This further illustrates the meaning and purpose of the alphabet. Have him decorate and color them.

Another approach to alphabet card-making is incorporating a picture within the writing of the letter. The picture should relate to that specific letter of the alphabet you are drawing. Make them funny and exaggerated.

That is, draw a big cobra snake in the shape of an *s* hissing for the letter *s*. Printed symbols triggered by visual memory are easier to remember.

Have your alphabet cards laminated and mounted. This gives them a place of permanence and importance. When mounting them, place them low enough for the child to see them clearly. Find 3-D representations of each letter of the alphabet, for example, a balloon, badge, and a button for the letter *B*. Do this for all the letters of the alphabet. When collected, place all objects into a big box and play "Mystery Grab." The object of the game is to simply grab an object from the box, name it, and tell what letter it begins with. At school, the kids love to dip into the box and pull out an object.

Another great game I found on the Internet and played with a group of young learners was "Blind Pick." It is similar to "Pin the Tail on the Donkey." To play this game, you need a large sheet of paper and colorful markers. On the sheet of paper, write the letters of the alphabet in mixed-up order and all over the page. Hang the paper at your child's eye and reach level, and blindfold him. Spin him around and have him point to a section on the paper. Take off the blindfold and have him tell you the letter he is pointing to.

Think of any favorite game you played as a child and modify it. These games are all fun to play with the family during those Family Nights. On Family Nights, play letter bingo, sing the Alphabet song, play the Candy Land game, or any game that teaches letter identification. Adapt, make, and play your own board games. Young writers delight in practicing writing the letters of the alphabet as they make and play the game.

When working on letter knowledge, teach letters sounds as well. An excellent beginning activity is to simply introduce your child to hand-held mirrors. Allow your child the opportunity to explore and see themselves in the mirror making different sounds. Have them make observations, and describe in detail what is happening to their mouth, tongue, jaw, lips, teeth, and so on when different movements are applied. Some children may feel awkward when looking at themselves. Others love to make silly expressions and watch themselves in the mirror.

Once they are quite comfortable with using the mirror and describing their observations, have them watch and recount what is happening as they say the letters of the alphabet. Talk about how the facial parts feel when different movements are applied:

- Discuss how the lips pucker together when saying *p* as in pink, are wide open when saying *a* as in apple, or stretched wide apart when saying *wh* as in whistle.

- Share thoughts and ideas about how the teeth rest on the lower lip when saying *v* as in *love*, how the tongue sits on the ridge behind the teeth when saying *dr* as in *dragon*, and pushes in between the upper and lower teeth when saying *th* as in *think*.
- Examine how the tongue touches the roof of the mouth when saying *ch* as in *church*, or hits the back of the mouth when saying *kick*, and how the sound comes from opening the back of your throat when saying *h* as in *house*.
- Have your child place his hands on the moving parts, have him feel the movement and vibrations. Have him focus at looking at and feeling the movements.

By the time many children have reached the preschool years, they may have had over a thousand books read to them. They have therefore seen and been exposed to print from the day they were born. They have already drawn, made signs, and scribbled their own writings. Children see print every time they turn on the television or the computer. They see print every time they take a walk to the store or go for a drive. Children face print every time they look through magazines, glance at a calendar, browse through the mail, open the refrigerator, or look into the kitchen cupboards or pantry. Seize the moment, and teach your child daily something that he did not know before. Make the written word a natural part of everyday life.

When practicing writing the actual letters of the alphabet, using reproducible worksheets is okay, as long as they are fun and not too overwhelming. I do encourage you though to think outside the box. Create different ways and methods of practicing the writing of the letters of the alphabet.

Erasing with water is an excellent activity that I saw a preschool teacher use. You need a chalk board or slate, paint brush, and a container of water. Write the letters of the alphabet that your child is learning with chalk on the board. Your child dips the paint brush in the water and "erases" your writing by tracing over what you have written.

Make an alphabet album. Take an old photo album, pictures from magazines or old books for each letter of the alphabet (may be two pictures per letter), and pre-made upper- and lowercase letter stickers. Place them inside the album in alphabetical order and equally spaced, using all he pages in the album. Hand your child a wipe-off marker and an old, preferably clean, sock. Let him trace the letters glued in the album again and again, using the sock as an eraser. It's guaranteed to be a favorite.

You can expose your child to the printed form by labeling many things that are a part of his environment. Together with your child, you can create a nameplate and put it on your child's bedroom door. You can do the same with the siblings' rooms. You can label anything from furniture, objects, or numbering the stairs. Invite questions about spelling. Demonstrate the spelling of the words that he wants to know. Spell his name for him, as well as the names of family members and pets. This helps to develop a spelling conscience at a very early age and helps to prepare the child for reading.

## CREATIVE PLAY

Encouraging creative play in your home makes for a positive environment. The sky is the limit. For example, you can create a post office, grocery store, restaurant, or even a travel agency; you can pretend play office, school, or doctor's office with your child. The more props you use, the better. When gathering old clothes and equipment for your child's creative play, remember to include writing and reading props such as old or used envelopes, writing paper, cards, pens, and pencils. When playing doctor's office, use your imagination and create appointment books and fill-out prescription sheets. You can design your own on the computer. Clocks, charts, diagrams, and magazines can be included as props.

*Econo-saver:* Go to restaurants, post offices, doctor's offices, and so forth, and ask if they have any old or outdated props or equipment to spare.

Fill your child's play world with cereal boxes, magazines, and calendars. Maps, signs, and old phone books are great, too, as are old and used cookbooks, catalogues, and newspapers. Fill the room with print everywhere and change the printed material often for variety.

## ROAD TRIPS

Exposure to print can be found everywhere, so you can take the learning on the road with trips to the grocery store, drug store, shopping mall, museum, science center, or library.

On warm and sunny days, take a trip to the zoo, the farmer's market, or the amusement park. Together, read and interpret the information signs and hands-on activity signs. Have fun sharing and reading together. You'll be amazed at what the kids can read and notice.

Believe it or not, the courthouse and government buildings are fascinating places for children, as well as police and fire stations. I've visited these places many times on field trips and outings with students from all grades. All the children have loved the experience and I have myself.

Make sure you take your kids with you when you visit the post office or have a doctor's or dentist's appointment. The more exposure to the world and print, the more inquisitive and eager your children will be.

Go to a pet store or the SPCA, and ask the employees about the different animals. Take a day trip to the country and visit a farm or petting zoo and talk to the people there. Visit a hotel, train, or bus station and ask someone to take you on a tour of the building. During the tour, discuss and use terms such as bellhop, porter, clerk, bus driver, tickets, and lobby.

The swimming pool, ball games, park, church, and theatre are great places to see and study writing. The ideas are limitless. Go ahead; take the risk and try them out.

It is important to surround your child with print. It encourages reading and makes print an automatic part of his day. Furthermore, it helps build word recognition and vocabulary, and fosters word association knowledge.

My husband, an environmentally conscious man, is very distraught by what he calls all the advertising "pollution." He hates all the billboards that "cover up nature," as he puts it. From an environmental point of view, this may indeed seem negative.

Nonetheless, children, who are naturally inquisitive and fascinated by advertising print, are automatically drawn to the print. They are sponges, soaking up whatever information is around them. Children, automatically and naturally, try to make sense of everything they see around them.

When your child asks you what the word "affordable" means because he has seen it in flashy bold print on the television screen, you realize the impact of advertising. How many times have you gone past a McDonald's restaurant only to have your pre-literate child read the McDonald's golden arches logo and say, "Let's go to McDonald's"?

Advertising print bombards children constantly. It only makes sense to turn this to your advantage. Have your child locate the writing and labeling of advertising signs. Collect various logos and messages and place them in a scrapbook as a reading reference for your child.

## FUN AND GAMES

You can create fun and easy environmental logo print games by adapting them to simple childhood games, such as the memory game. All you need are two identical sets of advertising logo flash cards.

You can make your own sets by using environmental print. Here are instructions on how to get this done: Cut out 20 to 40, 3 × 5" blank cards from bulletin board paper, card stock, or pre-cut index cards. Make sure all the cards are of the same size. Place a logo on each card. Remember to have double copies of each logo.

To play the game, shuffle all the cards from both sets together and place them face down. Each person takes a turn turning up two cards. The object of the game is to find a match. When a match is located, that person gets to keep the matching cards and takes another turn. When there is no match, the player must return the chosen cards to the pile face down. The next person takes his turn. The winner is the child with the most matches.

Any childhood game can be adapted to fit your needs. How about fishing for logos in a fishpond? To play this game, you must first draw and cut out a large number of fish shapes. You then paste a logo on the fish's body—one logo per fish. Attach a metal paper clip to each fish, and then have your child fish for logos using a homemade fishing rod. The fishing rod can be as simply made as a pencil with an attached string and a magnet for the hook. When your child catches a fish, he must identify the logo before getting to keep his catch.

How about "Go Fish?" To play the game, one needs duplicate sets of advertising logo flash cards. These can be handmade or copied from the computer. Make them durable by gluing them onto stock paper and laminating them. Shuffle the cards thoroughly and carefully. Deal each player three to five cards, depending on the numbers of players. Place the remaining cards face down and spread out in front of everyone, resembling a pond.

Each player gathers his or her cards and looks at them, making sure not to show anyone his or her hand. The first player (chosen by the group according to a highest roll of a dice, closest birthday, oldest person, etc.) begins by asking a certain player from the group for a specific card (logo). If that player does not have the requested card (logo), he must "Go Fish." The player must then draw a card from the fish pond. If, after doing so, the child has a match, he is to place that match down for everyone to see.

It is then his turn again. He continues to take a turn until he does not have a match from either the person beside him or from the center pile. This is when his turn ends, and it becomes the next person's turn. The winner is the child with the most matches.

Other childhood games to adapt and use are an Environmental Scavenger Hunt with logos, Hot and Cold, and I Spy. All you have to do is to think of any game that you loved to play as a child and see if you can change the rules to make it a letter identification game.

For example, you can tell a Rebus story with environmental print and pictures. Copy a child's favorite story or one he has dictated to you and replace some key words with applicable pictures. Try using only advertising logo pictures in this game.

Remember that children have a lot of background knowledge and understanding as far as environmental print goes. They see and hear logos and songs daily on television, radio, and through advertising. When children hear and see print, it focuses their attention to the importance of words. It helps them to build a vocabulary. Manipulating and focusing on environmental print certainly draws the attention of your child, and they start to understand the relationship between print and pictures.

## RAINY DAY ACTIVITIES

On those rainy, gloomy days when you can't or won't go outside, you can take this opportunity to bake cookie words using your favorite cookie recipe. Have your child make cookie letters from the alphabet.

To begin, pick your favorite cookie dough recipe and prepare a batch. When ready, roll the dough into a long snake and shape into different letters. Then bake as instructed in the recipe. Voila—you have cookie letters to enjoy. As a time saver, I found it useful to mix a batch of freezer dough in advance, so it is ready and available for baking at a moment's notice.

For breakfast and Pancake Tuesday, try making alphabet pancakes. Use your favorite secret pancake recipe. If your life is crazy like mine, don't be shy, go ahead and buy packaged pancake mix. That's the only kind of pancakes my kids have.

Now here's the writing pencil. Fill an empty and clean mustard or ketchup squeeze bottle with the pancake batter and cut the tip of the spout to the size you'd need for "writing." Write (squeeze) your letters onto a hot grill or fry pan and cook as usual.

It is fun for your child to fashion letters out of homemade dough, Jell-O Jigglers, or even a commercially prepared product such as Fimo. This is a fantastic clay-like product and comes in many wonderful colors, even fluorescent. It requires no mixing, is not messy, and easily bakes in a regular or toaster oven. Make sure the product is Fimo or oven friendly.

My daughter and I once tried to bake with what we thought was Fimo in the oven, only to find out it was modeling clay. Did you know modeling clay melts in the oven? We found out the hard way. What a mess. Believe me, it is nearly impossible to clean melted modeling clay off of a cookie sheet.

There are also sponge and stamp letters available on the market which can be used to make letters and simple words. Simply visit your favrotie scrapbooking store. Kids love to work with them. It is something they consider to be fun, different, and special.

Other ways to incorporate using and learning letters of the alphabet are:

- Help your child make his own gift wrap for presents by teaching him how to sponge print, "Happy Birthday" onto blank wrapping paper.
- Design some dough letter mobiles with your child. Create alphabet paper chains or pipe cleaner letters. The writing practice opportunities are endless.
- Create a collage of letters. In order to do this, gather all the old magazines that are lying around the house. Have your child find, cut, and paste all shaped letters, funky designs, uppercase and lowercase, interesting fonts. Paste them onto a large sheet of bulletin board paper.
- Plan a texture collage, providing him with scraps of material and different kinds of textured paper to cut out letters of the alphabet. Cut letters out of burlap, fleece, silk, sand paper, and scrapbooking paper. Label the top, right-hand corner of your paper with a letter of the alphabet. Cover the entire page with the letter. Paste them in any fashion all over the page. Include their own free-hand or stencil letters.

Afterward, discuss the different letters, their shape, and their level of difficulty in making them. Talk about curvy letters, tall letters, short letters, basement or tail letters, as well as their texture with your child. Repeat this activity by building spelling webs with different themes. Spelling webs are activities designed to build vocabulary. Start with a theme word(s); for example, "basement words." Place the word in the middle of the page in big bold letters. Brainstorm and add all words that have basement letters in there (i.e., han*g*, thin*g*, *app*le).

Build a sand or salt box. It is fun and easy to build. All you need is sand or salt and an old shoebox. Half fill the box with sand or salt, and shake it till it is level and smooth. Have your child practice making letters in the solution. When finished, simply erase (shake) the words.

Experiment with sand or glitter and glue lettering. Simply write letters with white glue on paper. Before the glue dries, sprinkle on sand or glitter. You can also use dry alphabet noodles and cereal letters. Mother Nature has a beautiful selection of objects to use: sea shells, feathers, twigs, dried leaves, and flowers and so on. How about secret letters with lemon juice and a flashlight? Together, you and your child squeeze fresh lemon juice into a glass, fill an eye dropper with the collected juice and write onto a blank piece of white paper several letters. Let the paper dry. The letters disappear. To read the letters darken the room and turn on the flashlight. See before your eyes the previously written letters.

Do you remember the old favorite, "All about me stories"? Have the children organize magazine pictures or actual photographs according to a specified theme, such as "Me, on my summer vacation," "My family and me," or "Things, I like to do." Then have your child tell you the story while you write the captions.

One day, when I was teaching a low-functioning student named Jay, I tried the photo album activity to stir his interest in writing. I gave him a camera and film (yes, in those days we used film). I taught him how to use it and let him take school pictures. I then had the film developed. Thank goodness today for digital cameras. It's a lot easier then the old-fashioned film camera. Later, I had Jay write captions beneath each picture to create an "All about me" story.

This activity turned out to be an excellent exercise. Not only did it increase his interest in writing, it also improved his writing skills. This exercise taught him that the printed word must be meaningful to the reader, and that in the writing process, there is a relationship between print and pictures.

For a special treat, Jay sometimes went to the principal's office and shared his photo album with him. That was a great bonding time for the principal and him, as Jay most often saw the principal when he was in trouble. From this activity, Jay learned that sharing one's writing can be an important part of the writing process and be fun at the same time—an added bonus.

Of course, always have alphabet puzzles, Spill and Spell, Go Fish, dominoes, Scrabble, lotto, and bingo games readily available. Electronic alphabet activity sets and computer programs are also a must in the process of working with your child.

Immersing your child in a print-enriched world is an important critical first step toward the beginnings of spelling awareness and mastery. Manipulating language in a meaningful and purposeful fashion provides all kinds of opportunities to jump-start your child's learning process.

The activities and suggestions in this chapter foster and encourage word knowledge and word understanding. They enhance word association and recognition skills. Increased knowledge about print and its function is guaranteed. Learning about the relationship between speech, print, pictures, and the real world is ensured. Your child's spoken and written vocabulary, as well as his listening and thinking skills improve. Your commitment to help your child, by providing him with a nurturing environment, fun games, and activities, aid in his curiosity for learning.

You, as a parent have become more knowledgeable about the spelling process, specifically the symbol-to-print concept. You have learned how to set up writing and reading centers for your child. You are more adept and self-assured at book and reading material selection. Your skills, confidence, and ability to facilitate your child's learning increase.

Continued time, effort, and purposeful activities prepare your child for higher levels of spelling development and comprehension. Your increased knowledge, understanding, and commitment are your child's escort into a new world of imagination.

# CHAPTER 2

# Primary/Kindergarten— Early Grade 1

## Spelling Background Knowledge: Word Concept

During this level of spelling, young spellers have advanced in their knowledge of writing to include the concept of a word. They are cognizant of the fact that writing is made up of letters and when strung together, those letters make words. They understand that pictures are not writing. They have advanced beyond the symbol and picture stage. They further know that letters have certain sounds associated with them, albeit they are inexperienced in their ability to break down a word into its sounds on account of the complexity of the sound-to-letter procedure.

Children, at this stage of spelling development, however, are unable to hold the word they are trying to spell long enough in their minds to complete the task of sound-to-letter spelling that makes up a word. It is usually the first and last sound/letter combination that is recorded.

Throughout this developmental phase, children use inventive and abbreviated spelling when writing their ideas. They are aware that people write using some kind of spelling standard. They realize that each letter has an associated sound and that words are made up of specific letter and sound combinations. Children choose groups of letters or even single letters for their word spelling. The letters chosen are the ones they hear (sound) when articulating the word. Thus, the spelling of words often consists of a grouping of incomplete or inaccurate attempts at sound-to-letter

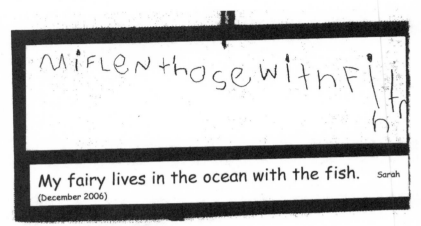

**Figure 2.1.    Sarah's writing sample**

spelling (phonics). They may or may not be aware of the left-to-right reading/print sequence.

Your child, when spelling at this stage, is attempting to put together the letters of the alphabet and learning how to write them, as well as figuring out how the mouth, jaw, and tongue move when saying them and how they correlate to the sounds.

Sarah has written a story about a fairy that lives in the ocean (see figure 2.1). You can see that with her writing, she is clearly recognizing the beginning sound-to-letter representation: *mi* (my) *f* (fairy) *l* (lives) *en* (in) *th* (the) *ose* (ocean) *with* (with) *fitrn* (fish). She knows that words are written with letters and not pictures; she also knows that the letters must represent the sounds she hears, and she is aware of left-to-right writing standards. What she still needs to experiment with are the syllables (beginning, middle, and ending sounds) and word boundaries. Even at this early stage, her writing is readable within context and is logical and sequential.

Kegan's writing uses similar principles as Sarah's (see figure 2.2). She is writing down the letters that make the sounds she hears when saying the story in her head. *Mu* (my) *frs* (fairy's) *n* (name) *is* [omission] *sp* (sparkle), *she* [omission] *lfs* (lives) *n* (in) *the* [omission] *ro* (rainbow), *she* [omission] *fs* (flies) *r* (really) *y* (well). Two important observations to note regarding her sounding out techniques: the *f* sound she hears in *lives* and the *y* sound she hears in *well*. The *y* sound is interpreted by the way the mouth moves

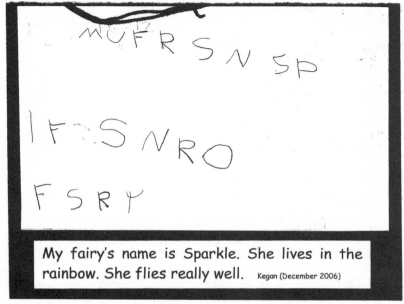

My fairy's name is Sparkle. She lives in the rainbow. She flies really well.    Kegan (December 2006)

**Figure 2.2.   Kegan's writing sample**

when it says the letter *y* and not by the sound the letter makes. This is very common at this stage of spelling development.

Always respect your child's first writings as they are ideas in progress. Children in this stage of spelling development need to be treated and respected as complete and full writers, filled with wonderful and interesting ideas. They need to feel fully competent and at ease when putting their ideas down permanently on paper through their scribbles, inventive spelling, and pictures. They need to be assured and successful in the knowledge that their writing can be read by themselves and others, perhaps with their help and a little imagination.

# Reading Ideas and Activities

When developing and encouraging word awareness with emergent writers, it is important for you to choose specific activities that foster this endeavor. As is mentioned many times throughout this book, it is imperative to keep the activities fun and engaging, yet purposeful. This is not a time to keep them busy. It is a time for you and your child. Enjoy it, treasure it. Together, engage in a lot of talk about words. Constantly build on his or her vocabulary base. Read, read, and read more. Have you heard that one from me before? Trust me; there is no greater way to demonstrate the power of a word than reading. See chapter 1 for reading ideas and activities. The same book preparations, talks, predictions for pre-reading, reading, and post-reading activities used in chapter 1 are to be considered a must.

# Writing Ideas and Activities

### WORD MODELING

Modeling can provide the conversation point to engage beginning writers and spellers. It also provides the beginning writer with a visual and functional understanding of writing. Children need to see that we value writing and use this medium as a means of communicating. Be a public writer. Place different types of writing notes in your office, computer area, or desk. Keep thank you note cards, blank note cards, occasional cards, and all different kinds of stationery.

*Econo-saver*: Recycle old and used occasional cards you receive throughout the year for your child to write on and use to send his or her own personal greetings. Cut them up into smaller cards. Kids love choosing their own card.

It is also a plus to involve your child with answering e-mails. Engage your children in the writing process by simply announcing that you are about to write and then actually talk about the writing in the process. Use words like: word, sentence, letter, sound, punctuation, and so forth. It helps to sometimes spell out loud and describe how the letters are formed. This grants your child permission to observe and make self-discoveries about letter formation, patterns, and combinations within a communicative meaningful context. Encourage your child to write his own letter to enclose with your message. Showcasing your interest and curiosity about the formation and meaning of words has a positive impact on your child's progress.

## WORD BUILDING

It is beneficial to have beginning writers practice standard writing using their own names. This helps ease the path from scribbling to writing and is personally meaningful. Furthermore, it provides the first memorized models of word making and gives the child tremendous power over his writing.

Providing realistic opportunities is simple: begin with the child's name. His name can be used in a variety of meaningful ways. Have your child always write his name on all samples of his work. Chore lists and charts are also good places to perform this process.

A word of caution: be careful with your encouragement. You may have your child writing his name on everything with any kind of writing medium. Set some guidelines. I can see it now, the mirror covered with Johnny's name (several times) in red lipstick. Oh dear!

How about having children make their own bedroom door sign with foam paper? After printing or cutting out their names, allow them to decorate it. Cut a hole at the top, one big enough to hang on the doorknob and voilà—you have a bedroom door sign.

Have your child make her own placemat for crafts or for table setting. Together, you and your child purchase some heavy duty and durable plain material. Cut it in the shape of a placemat with pinking-shears. With fabric pens, have your child write his or her name and design the placemat.

Here's another idea: making name plates for your child's room or work space. They can be as elaborate as painted wooden plaques and letter blocks made with Daddy and Grandpa's help or as simple as a construction paper plaque, with the child's name written using shreds of bright and colorful construction paper collaged together to form each of the individual letters.

With whatever activity you choose to use, it is imperative to involve your child in the process. Make it fun and exciting with fancy paper (scrapbooking paper, construction paper, foam paper, and even mirror paper), funky material (burlap, fleece, and felt), and you can even label with a label machine. I have a label machine that my girls and students love to use.

*Econo-saver*: Think beyond standard paper. Visit wallpaper stores and ask for old and out of circulation wall paper samples. Visit fabric stores or wood supply stores, and shop in the bargain bins.

It is not hard to provide a variety of writing tools for the child. Include slates, white boards, computers, Etch-a-Sketch, stencils, letter stickers, pens, pencils (colored and regular), pads of different colors, shapes, and textured paper.

Once you have the writing tools, you can build words on paper, build words using magnetic letters on metal cookie sheets or wooden blocks, and even build words in a tray of sand, salt, or flour. Cut words out of sand paper, make them from gel, finger-paint, shaving cream, mud, pipe cleaners, clay, toothpicks, popsicle sticks or snow—anything you can imagine. How about some edible words formed with whipped cream, peanut butter, and pudding? Think touchable, visual, and kinesthetic. Create crayon resist words, mosaic words, stencil letter words, sponge painting words, tissue paper words, and vegetable print words.

Word Designer Activity is an easy and engaging activity for all children. Begin by having on hand several different kinds of writing utensils (such as pencils, markers, crayons, pastels, coloring pencils), different kinds of fun paper (construction, Bristol board foam paper, for example),

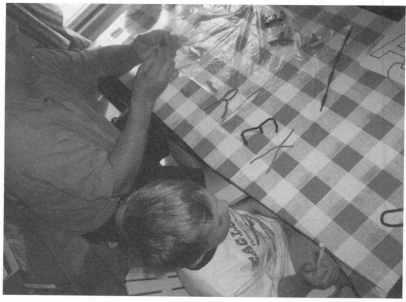

**Figure 2.3.   Alexander and Dad**

a word card collection, and large stencils (5–10 cm). Using the word card as a model, have your child re-write the words he sees using the stencils. Once the word is copied, you can use a variety of colors, shapes, and designs to vertically, horizontally, and diagonally decorate the inside of the word.

*Econo-saver*: A good and cheap way to store materials is to use good old baggies with zippers, old baby-wipe containers, and old plastic containers. Label them with permanent markers. The trick now becomes to train your child to put things away, properly, in their rightful container. I personally haven't figured that one out, yet.

The important thing is to be creative. For example, talk about the shapes of the letters in the words. Take a marker and draw around the word. Let them see the tall shapes, middle shapes, and the ones that drop to the basement. Focusing on word shapes helps build visual memory and recognition. When the child hears the word being spoken, he uses his visual memory and "sees" the shape and the number of letters that make up the word in his mind, thus becoming better able to chunk the sound of the word into the correct letters.

When combining several words together to introduce the idea of basic sentences, the best way is to take simple books with limited words per page, read them, play word games with them, copy them, and manipulate them. Try writing down the words from the book on large-sized fun paper. Cut the words out, study them, talk about them, and replace them in story order.

Another option is to play a game of Hide and Seek. Hide one word and see if they can guess which word is missing. I have found this type of game to be most successful when you omit nouns and verb words that the child is already familiar with and then move on with the more abstract words.

Familiar and memorized nursery rhymes and poems are great for chanting and exploring together. For this purpose, write them down on chart paper. You and your child can read them together and track the words with your finger, all the while engaging in conversation about words and what they look like.

Take the time to rebuild rhymes and poems. Start by choosing a poem, copy the verses onto a sheet of chart paper, cut out the stanzas, and have your child match the cutouts with the original copy.

Create a game using old nursery rhymes to practice name writing. Just copy the rhyme as usual and substitute familiar family and friends' names for the textbook name. See how much fun you'll have reading and reciting the new nursery rhymes.

There are many games you can play to assist your child's learning. Search the Internet, visit an educational store, or subscribe to an educational/activity magazine. Here's an old game with a modified twist: Who stole the cookies from the cookie jar?

Start off with writing out the following verse on a large piece of chart paper: "Who stole the cookies from the cookie jar? Was it you (*person's name*)? Who me? Yes, you? Couldn't be. Then who? Was it you (*person's name*)?" Then, on separate cue cards, write each of the names of your child's friends and family members. Place the cards in a cookie jar and mix them up.

You are now ready to play the game. Begin by familiarizing yourself with the verse by singing it a few times without drawing from the cookie jar. When comfortable with the verse, get ready to draw from the jar. Begin by singing the verse. When you get to the "who stole the cookie from the cookie jar? Was it you (*person's name*)?" part, draw a name from the jar and have your child read the name and practice writing that person's name. Do not overload the jar or the child with too many names. Three or four familiar names are fine to start with.

Similar name writing games can be creatively put together with ever-enduring nursery rhymes such as It's Raining, It's Pouring. Use a rain hat to hold the cue cards and sing: "It's raining, it's pouring, and (*person's name*) is snoring; He (she) bumped his (her) head on the side of the bed, and couldn't get up in the morning." Other name-including nursery rhymes that come quickly to mind are: Pat-a-cake, Davy, Davy Dumpling, and Little Jack Horner.

As you see, these rhymes are not that hard to come up with. A little research on the Internet is sure to provide you with more than enough nursery rhymes to modify and work with. Do similar activities with simple songs. Be creative and innovative.

How about honing and practicing your story telling abilities? Practice and rehearse the retelling of old-fashioned, tried-and-true fairy tales. Practice using lots of excitement and exaggeration in your voice, face, and hands. When you feel confident, re-tell the story to your child. After the re-telling, you can print out important words from the story and practice word building.

## WORD SORT

Word sorting activities are great to introduce and teach your child about word recognition and word formation. There are lots of games you can play to enhance their learning. The following are some examples:

### Ransom Word Treasure Hunt

Random Word Treasure Hunt is always a fun activity. This is how it works: Cut out or make words with different fonts from old magazines, newspapers, computer printouts, and different types of font stencils. Many card and craft stores have all kinds of letter stickers of various fonts. Have your child sort the words. As children identify words in differing cases and fonts, they become better able to recognize letters in new contexts.

### World Word Short Search

Start by determining what word category to use (fruits, nouns, alphabet, colors, etc.). Then together with your child, look around your environment, call out names of objects and record the words that come to mind and fit your category on paper. For example, if the category happens to be "the alphabet," have your child call out (items) words she sees and can think of that begin with the different letters of the alphabet (such as *A*: apple, *B*: bed, *C*: chair, *D*: doughnuts). Copy those words down neatly in large print, there after have your child cut them out and glue them on paper. When this task is complete, have them circle the individual words with pen or string.

### Not Like the Other One

Put together a collection of words (50–60) in advance. Next, have your child sort the words according to some kind of category (not necessarily using all the cards; she needs to have at least three in her category). Your job is to determine and guess your child's category strategy (for example, mop, mat, and man—words that start with the letter m). Switch roles with your child and play again.

### Word Clothesline

Word Clothesline is always fun for the little one. Take your word card collection and do the same activity as described above in Not Like the Other One, only this time have your child clothespin the cards onto the clothesline (a piece of string tied across the room) into some word-sort category. Same as last time, you guess her word sort strategy and change roles.

### A Giant Picture Word Sort

Choose a particular theme (dinosaurs, space, or spring, for example) and draw a large picture of something that identifies your theme. Cut it out and add any needed specific detailing. Using a pencil, dictionary, and topic-related resources, find words that match the topic. Print the words randomly, yet neatly on the large picture. Have your child trace the words with crayons or markers and display them on the wall or refrigerator door.

## RAINY DAY ACTIVITIES

On those rainy, gloomy days, it's fun to stay in and bake cookie words using your favorite cookie recipe. Try warming up some hot chocolate and delving into homemade cookie letters and words.

*Econo-saver*: An inexpensive and easy way to always have cookie dough on hand is to mix a batch of freezer dough in advance. That way it is ready and available at a moment's notice.

*Econo-saver*: Make a batch of either self-hardening or oven-baked dough. Store it in zip-lock bags and remove all the air. Then place the bags in plastic containers with lids. Search the Internet for recipes.

There are also sponge letters available on the market. You can use them to make labels for objects and items found around the home. Help your child make his own gift wrap for presents. Have him sponge print, "Happy Birthday" onto blank wrapping paper.

To create another fun activity for your child, make words by cutting out letters from newspapers, magazines, and even fancy paper from scrapbooking.

Write your words on graph paper and trace the shapes of the letters. Talk to your child about tall letters, short letters, and basement letters while you are tracing the shapes. Outline them with crayons and string, yarn, or glitter and glue. Make it entertaining and interesting, a fun day for child and parent. Practice writing the word with alphabet pasta or Alphabits. Glue it on paper and hand the note to the other parent, grandparent, or sibling.

It is also fun to design dough-word mobiles with your child or creating jewelry names and save them for gifts. How about making name tags out of either kind of dough, decorating them, and placing them on presents instead of bows? The possibilities are endless.

Here are some more rainy day activities ideas:

### Designing Word Collages

Children love to cut and paste and love to find funky stylized print. Gather old magazines.

*Econo-saver:* Begin a collection of old magazines. You'll be forever using them while your child is in school. You can always collect used magazines from friends and neighbors, but don't forget to approach your local drug store or bookstore to get free unsold, outdated ones.

*Econo-saver:* Think about permanent and easily accessible storage of messy and heavy magazines. You may want to purchase a plastic bin with lid, or you may want to file them according to themes in storage boxes. My mom, a teacher too, had an entire filing cabinet filled with old magazines. They were all organized according to subject. It was great to use whenever I had a school project.

Have your child find and cut out words from old recycled magazines. Label the top, right-hand corner of chart paper with a letter of the alphabet. Cover and paste the entire page with words your child has found that begin with the same letter you've written at the top of the page. Paste them in any fashion all over the page.

To further challenge your child, provide him with material scraps and paper of all kinds of texture. Have him make words from free-hand or with stencils onto the material scraps. Cut them out and paste them on the large sheets of bulletin board. Sit with your child and discuss the different words and their relationships, their shapes, as well as their textures. Repeat the same activity, building spelling webs with different themes. For example, you can use favorite holiday words, seasonal words, or feeling words.

To further make this project interesting and challenging, you can experiment with sand, salt, soap bubbles, or glitter and glue lettering. Simply write words or messages with white glue on paper. Before the glue dries, sprinkle on sand or glitter. Attempt the same activity with dried alphabet noodles and cereal letters. There are so many ways to play the letter game. You can draw, cut, and/or print your own words, for example.

### Secret Messages

Here's what you need: some lemon juice, white paper, a cotton swab, and an iron. Dip the cotton swab into the lemon juice and use it to write your secret message on the white piece of paper. Let it dry. Together, with your help, place a warm iron on the picture. See what happens when heat from the iron is applied to the secret message.

### Dictionary Scrapbook of Words

Begin by dividing the pages according to the number of pages in your scrapbook and the alphabet. Place each letter of the alphabet on the top, left corner, using both upper- and lowercase script. Enter the words your child uses daily, alphabetically. Whenever possible, provide a picture. Remember though, use and build words that are nouns and verbs. It is so much easier to relate with pictures than abstract adjectives.

### Student Word Book

A student word book is a working student dictionary. Within its pages are pre-written high frequency words and blank lines for future additional words. The student comes to you for a spelling of a word, and it is recorded in the book.

After gaining some knowledge with scrapbook words, introduce a student word book. To make one, purchase a scribbler and divide pages evenly according to each letter of the alphabet (like an address book). Label appropriate pages with the letters of the alphabet. Gather a list of high-frequency words from the Internet and write them permanently into the book. In the back include a listing of colors, numbers, months of the year words, family member names, and any other frequently used word collections from your child's environment. You now have a student word book. Your child is ready to begin to record his entries.

## Word Wall of Fame

Another activity includes building and creating a Word Wall of Fame, a systematically organized collection of words displayed in large clear-print letters on a wall or other large display area.

Purchase a large cork board, four by two feet, like the ones used in bulletin boards, and place it on your child's bedroom wall. Decorate it with a bright and cheerful boarder. Place printed letters of the alphabet horizontally across the board. Remember to use both upper- and lowercase letters of the alphabet. Beneath each letter, vertically place cards with words your child uses in his vocabulary—high-frequency words.

Each time your child wants to add a new word, add it to the Word Wall of Fame. Children love adding new words to the Word Wall of Fame. Encourage your child to refer to it when practicing writing. For those of you who have limited space, a portable word wall on a shower curtain, a folding tri-fold, or even brochure-sized ones are great. If you are crafty and have lots of time, think about creating a quilt Wall of Fame with the alphabet letters (upper- and lowercase) stitched onto the quilt; place Velcro strips in columns beneath each of the alphabet letters. Print daily used and high-frequency words from your child's writing on sturdy Bristol board and on the backside; place the other side of the Velcro strips. You now have an extraordinary educational writing tool for your child, as well as an exquisite keepsake of her childhood.

There are many word-wall games and activities you can play. Children enjoy playing "Who Am I?"

## "Who Am I?"

Here is how to play this game: Give three clues about a word from the Word Wall of Fame. The first clue is always, "It's one of the words from your word wall." After giving all three clues say, "Who am I?" The child must then copy down the word he thinks is from the word wall.

## Word-Wall Cheer

Word-Wall Cheer is another great game I played with my students. I've modified it for you. Choose five words from the Word Wall of Fame. You call out the first letter of a word. Your child copies down the letter. Each consecutive letter is named by you and your child copies down the letters until the entire word is spelled. Finally, spell the word out loud together in a cheerleader fashion.

### Bees in the Behive

I spent a few weeks in a grade-2/3-combined classroom with sixty kids and two teachers. I learned this game from them. All the word-wall words were taken down and placed in a papier-mâché beehive. The students sat in a circle and each took a word from the beehive. If they were able to read the word they got to keep it. If they could not, the word was returned to the beehive. If they pulled a card with the word *buzz* from the box, all the cards they had collected had to be returned to the beehive. It stings when that happens. The student at the end of the game with the most cards was declared the winner. This game can easily be adapted for small and paired groupings. Just modify the number of cards in the beehive.

### Word-Wall Hopscotch

This game is particularly fun when the kids are stuck indoors and need to get active. You will need to gather the following: an old (but clean) shower curtain liner with a hopscotch board drawn on in black permanent marker (label it 1-10), a set of word-wall words, and a bean bag.

Divide the class into two teams. The youngest person throws the bean bag into square 1 (okay to just drop it) and reads the word-wall word correctly that is drawn from the deck. That person must then hop all the way to the end of the game board, turn around, and hop back. Single squares like 1, 4, and 7 must be hopped on with one foot. Double squares like 2 and 3, 5 and 6, and 8 and 9, must be straddled with one foot in each square simultaneously.

When a player completes his turn successfully, he gives the marker to the next person on his team. That person throws the bean bag into square 2 and proceeds to repeat the above directions, but skipping over square 2 this time since it now holds the marker. This continues, advancing one square at a time and passing the bean bag to a new player each time until someone from that team makes an error. Reading the word-wall card incorrectly, not skipping the square with the bean bag, hopping on any lines, or skipping squares constitutes an error and begins team 2's turn.

The winner is the team who can progress through the numbers 1 to 10 and back again. Just a word of caution: please have the players play this game in their bare feet, otherwise they can slip very easily. The game can be played at home with the family. My girls' grandpa did—psst—he's seventy-six years old.

### Around the World in Words

My students absolutely love playing this game at the end of the day while they wait for the bell to go home. They often request it. It's quick, simple, and easy to start. All the students sit in their desks. The teacher appoints one student to stand behind another student who is sitting in their desk. The teacher flashes them a word-wall word. Whichever child says the word first moves besides the next student. The student who makes it back to his or her own desk first is the winner. Come on, moms, I know you can modify this game for your family.

*Econo-saver*: As you can see, you have now become a saver of everything. Set up an extra box for your recycling, labeled "crafts." When everyone is recycling, encourage them to place clean and dry products you are in need of into the craft box. On a weekly basis, place a list of items you need and are collecting on the outside of the box.

*Econo-saver*: Find storage areas in your garage or basement. You can buy file boxes from a moving company or, even better, ask your partner to bring unused and unclaimed paper boxes with lids from the office. You can even ask for paper boxes at your child's school. They'll gladly give them away. Label the outside of the boxes and store them. They are just the right size for business-sized files.

## FAMILY NIGHT ACTIVITIES

Remember those family night gatherings from the previous chapter? Introduce spelling word games, homemade, commercially prepared, and modified "old favorites": Name and Word Bingo, Word Concentration, Word Memory, Hangman, Word Searches, Crosswords, Word Tic-Tac-Toe, Snap, Dominoes, Go-Fish, Spill and Spell, Boggle, and Scrabble quickly come to mind.

*Econo-saver:* A quick and effective way of collecting these wonderful games is by asking for them as birthday or Christmas presents from friends and relatives.

How about turning off all the lights and closing all the blinds in the living room? In the darkened room, use a flashlight to trace and make words on the wall.

Get together with your child to make invitations, thank you notes, birthday cards, and so forth. Encourage your child to write out grocery lists, calendar events, and chore notes. Keep in mind that it's the process of attempting writing that is important, not the correct spelling outcome.

Remember your story-telling practices. Here's the time to perform. As an added feature, purchase a small tri-fold, cover it in felt, and voilà—you have a felt board for story telling. Make and cut out characters and scenes from felt fabric about your story, always together with your child. While you are retelling the story, have your child also retell, by adding the characters and having them interact as the story progresses. Change roles and retell again. This keeps everyone involved.

One rewarding family writing activity is the family journal. This is simply an activity where one records important family dates and events. Have each family member tell memorable tidbits of information. As parents, you'll have to be responsible for the "limits." Some children could have field days on things that siblings would rather forget than remember. Let an older child be a younger child's scribe.

You can set a special time each day/night for journal writing. If it is too time-consuming on a daily basis, opt for weekly scheduling. Whichever way you choose to do this, just make sure that it is done regularly.

This is a wonderful activity for the family. It grants an opportunity to reflect, as a family, on the day's/week's events. It permits your child to write and express his thoughts in a safe and comfortable environment. Most importantly, it provides your child with lasting memories of his youth or at least an opportunity to abuse him at his wedding reception!

## QUICK PENCIL AND PAPER ACTIVITIES

Quick pencil and paper activities you can do while waiting at appointments or during that eternal wait for your other child to finish his activity are word searches, crosswords, word-webbing, and word poems. Consequently, never leave the house without a full file.

## Word Searches and Crosswords

Word searches and crosswords can easily be run off the computer beforehand using various themes and special interest words. You can use premade worksheets or create your own ones using words from your child's writing and lessons.

## Word-Webbing

Word-webbing is an activity with the goal to build vocabulary. In the middle of a blank sheet of paper, simply write a word, circle the word, brainstorm, and then write all the words, adjectives, thoughts, and memories associated with the word. Connect each word with the central word by drawing a line. When one subword is circled and a new and related word is mentioned, write it down too, circle it, and connect it to the subword. Continue this activity until all ideas are exhausted. See what kind of a web you have created.

## Writing Poetry

Writing poetry is also fun. The easiest and most exciting word poems for children to write are acrostic poems. The initial letter of the lines in the poem spells out a word or a name in vertical fashion. Take each letter and write a word, horizontally, that relates to the key word that is written vertically. Repeat with all letters in the key word. When you have finished, you have an acrostic poem.

Other poems for young children to write and experiment with the concept of words are word couplets. A word couplet is a four-lined poem where the last word of the first and the last lines rhyme. The theme of the poem should be an object of some sort.

Sensory poems are written using the five senses (sight, sound, touch, smell, and taste) as themes. The use of senses makes the writing come alive.

To begin writing the poem, warm-up by brainstorming and listing on paper several objects and their related emotions. Then follow a six-line format. The first line names the object and where you were at the time of the sighting of the object. Then each subsequent line describes the emotion you have about the object using: sounds like, smells like, tastes like, looks like, and feels like. When all senses are included, your child has created a sensory poem.

Other poetry ideas include cinquain—a favorite form of poetry writing for young writers. It is a five-line poem. The first line is made up of one word, a subject or noun. The second line is made up of two adjectives describing the subject or noun in line one. The third line is made up of adjectives describing the noun or subject in line one. The fourth line is made up of four words or a complete sentence describing the writer's feelings toward the subject or noun in line one. The fifth line is the same word repeated from the first line or a synonym of that word.

Five *W*'s nonrhyming poems are also quick and easy. Each line of the poem answers one of the 5 *W*'s: Who? What? When? Where? And Why? Line 1: Who is the poem about? Line 2: What action is happening? Line 3: When does the action take place? A time: season, past, or future. Line 4: Where does the action take place? Setting. Line 5: Why does this action happen? A reason. Poetry writing does not get any easier than this. There are many different styles of poetry writing to explore when working with words. Research the Internet, visit the library, or talk to your child's teacher for ideas.

Before leaving the house for your appointment, fill a bag or car pocket caddy with pencil and paper activities. Don't forget to include a white board and marker, as well as a great book. The carefree ride and waiting time is magnificent.

*Econo-saver*: Car Pocket Caddy—simply make a car pocket caddy out of sturdy material with straps attached to place around the headrest of the seat in front of where your child sits. This ensures easy accessibility for them while in the car, and is also easy for you to untie and take with you to any appointment.


## JOURNALING

Journals represent a private and uninterrupted time for reflection and expressing thoughts, ideas, worries, dreams, and wishes. It is a time when spelling, punctuation, and grammar are not the focus. Let your children express themselves with journal writing without the demand they typically have when doing assignments. This ensures a positive, stress-free and enjoyable time to experiment with writing. It is not meant to be a structured activity, which we are graded on or something we are made or told to do in a certain way.

With a fancy or cool unlined journal, have your child practice word lettering every day, using what they know about spelling and the construction of words. Let them know that this is their journal for daily writing. Prepare them prior to writing. Get their writing juices flowing. Talk about events that are important to them and have recently happened. Ask your child what they know about the subject matter they want to write about. Depending on her writing skill, allow her to draw and make sure you record her ideas down on paper. Have her write simple one word captions to go along with the picture. Provide writing prompts as guidelines and idea starters; many are available on the Internet.

At any time, when your child asks for spelling help, always encourage and give them a chance to put down the letters they feel make up the word and give it their best try, before you help them. Always applaud those best tries. Always remember that attempted "best" spellings are not wrong and are not indicators of failure to spell conventionally; consider them important vehicles toward reaching conventional spelling. A child's spelling reflects their current knowledge of sounds and written language conventions.

Be aware of your child's creativity and never confine spelling to formal instruction. Nevertheless, in saying this, I do not mean to say that you should forget that spelling is not learned through osmosis or incidentally. As a matter of fact, it is important to keep this in mind. It is a language-based activity, the development of which is dependent on many of the same intellectual and logistic processes as reading, listening, and speaking.

Spelling competency is a long-term evolution best achieved through an inquiry-based, practical, and purposeful manner that includes comprehensive language proficiency. It is of the essence to explore the spelling process in nurturing situations, where the teaching and manipulation of language is emphasized.

Informal experiences and practice with writing and spelling foster a beginning cognitive structure on which eventual standard spellings develop. Allow and encourage your children to write. Permit them to experiment and create their own spelling. Children must be given lots of opportunities to apply their developing understanding of orthographic knowledge in a variety of situations.

Immerse children in written language experiences and word study daily. Always let them share their writing with an audience and always encourage their writing. These opportunities should include observation, verification, as well as the revision and correction of spellings.

# CHAPTER 3

# Early Elementary

## Spelling Background Knowledge: Sound and Pattern Concept

At the sound and pattern concept stage of spelling development, the child has some basic sight word vocabulary and is exposed to print regularly. The child is a beginning reader and is well immersed and experienced with inventive spelling, making his predictions based on spelling knowledge and experience. Children are aware of sound to letter relationships and can reproduce most or all of the sounds they hear. In addition, children include long vowels in their spelling, because they can hear the long vowels when saying the word.

Children at this stage of spelling development are often not completely self-assured with all letter and sound representations. For letter sounds they are unsure of, children use mouth movement to predict the best spelling. As an example, children could spell *setting* and *sending* exactly the same way, because when concentrating only on how your mouth moves and ignoring the differences in the air flow, they appear the same.

Short vowels are chosen again by determining the letters that best represent the mouth movement when sounding out the word. Thus, the letters *a*, *i*, and *e* are often used interchangeably.

Silent letters, nasal letters (*m*'s and *n*'s—letters pronounced by pushing air out from the nose and not the mouth) are not recognized by "mouth-motion" spellers. Oftentimes neither are vowels in unstressed syllables because they are hard to hear and distinguish.

Due to the fact that these spellers, at this stage of spelling develop-ment, are still one sound per one letter spellers, they have difficulty with consonant blends and consonant digraphs. Oftentimes, these spellers will try to match the sound to a single letter and miss the blend or di-graph altogether. Other times, they will attempt a two letter combina-tion incorrectly.

Consonant blends are when two or more consonants run into one an-other or blend together, while maintaining their individual sounds. For ex-ample: blanket, plastic, treat, stripe, and grand. With consonant blends, it is usually *dr* and *tr* blends that children have difficulty hearing. When we pronounce these specific consonant blends in everyday speech, we do not say *t-ried* or *d-ragon*, we blend them together. Go figure. Children are no exception. Furthermore, because children still rely on mouth shape and movement, they often print *ch* for the consonant blend *tr* and *gr* or *jr* for the consonant blend *dr*.

Similar difficulty arises for children when spelling with digraphs. A con-sonant digraph is a group of two consonants that together make only one sound. For example chat, what, phone, and ghost. The two letters *c* and *h*, *w* and *h*, *p* and *h*, and *g* and *h*, when put together, form a unique sound.

Furthermore, children, at this level of spelling development, en-counter difficulty understanding that different sounds may be represented by the same letter or string of letters. For instance, the *ch* digraph found in the words: character, chorus, chauffer, chute, choir, chimp and chain, have four different sounds respectively: *k*, *sh*, *kw*, and *ch*.

Children are aware of plurals and past tenses and sometimes include word endings in their spellings. Most often these endings are added ac-cording to their phonetic sounds and not to word meaning or knowledge. The word *dressed* could be spelled *drest*, and *peaches* could be spelled *pechez*, and *ran* could be spelled *runned*.

Children at this stage of spelling development are experimenting with and aware of word boundaries and spacing. They also use upper- and low-ercase spelling with left-to-right progression more correctly.

Sophie's story reads like this: *wts* (Once) *th* (there) *was* [omission] *a* [omission] *fere* (fairy) *nat* (named) *Vilit* (Violet). *She* (She) *w* (was) *a* (a) *flwr* (flower) *fere* (fairy). *She* (She) *l* (likes) *to* (to) *sml* (smell) *the* (the) *feres* (flowers) (see figure 3.1).

Sophie is using spelling conventions commonly found at this level of spelling development. She is still spelling using the mouth-to-motion strategy

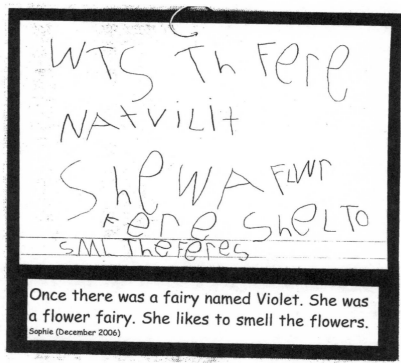

Once there was a fairy named Violet. She was a flower fairy. She likes to smell the flowers.

Sophie (December 2006)

**Figure 3.1.   Sophie's writing sample**

and is recording what her mouth does when saying the words: *wts* and *once*, *th* and *there*, *sm* and *smell*, and *Vilit* and *Violet*. In all three attempts, Sophie is using her mouth as a guide to spelling the letters she chooses to reproduce.

Furthermore, she is attempting to use vowels in her writing: *fere* and *fairy*, as well as *Vilit* and *Violet*. Notice that the word *flowers* is spelled two different ways: *flwr* and *feres*. Sophie may be experimenting with her vowel inclusions or she may have gotten mixed up with her spelling of *fairy*.

Sophie seems to be aware of left-to-right writing sequence as is noticeable with her story. She most often uses word spacing in her writing. The exceptions are "named Violet" and "she likes to."

Upper- and lowercase letters are used randomly throughout her writing. This is an indication of upper- and lowercase knowledge, but use and accuracy remains inconsistent.

**Figure 3.2a.    Sarah's writing sample**

In Sarah's writing sample (see figures 3.2a and b), many of the same strategies are noticeable and applied. Sarah has left-to-right progression figured out; notice the strategy her teacher and she are using to guide her writing and learning, namely the *X*s on each new line.

Sarah is using invented spelling to write, including the letters that make the sounds she feels when moving her mouth: *wints* for *once*, *livd* for

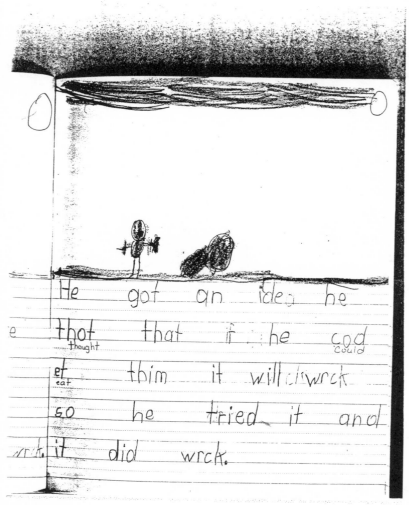

He got an idea he
<sub>e</sub> thot that if he cod
thought                          could
et thim it will dwrck
eat
so he tried it and
wrck it did wrck.

**Figure 3.2b.**

*lived, onder* for *under, grawnd* for *ground,* and *wr* for *were.* Consequently, she also omits silent letters that are not pronounced, as in *cod* for *could* and *thot* for *thought.*

Sarah is aware of past tenses and is trying to include them in her writing as in *livd* for *lived* and *namde* for *named.* The spelling of *ondr* for *under* and *wr* for *were* tells me that she hasn't developed the understanding of syllables and their position in writing.

As with Sophie, Sarah is attempting to add vowels in her writing. Sarah is aware of short vowel sounds as in *got* for *got, that* for *that,* and *will* for *will,* but is not consistently successful when choosing which vowel sound to write, as in the case of *thim* for *them.*

Sarah is consistently using her upper- and lowercase spelling rules correctly, has solid word boundaries, and has a set of sight word spellings to draw from.

Realize, understand, and credit the tremendous effort and skill that goes into spelling. When spelling, your child is attempting to put together letters of the alphabet to represent the sounds he hears.

Spelling attempts begin first with figuring out how the mouth, jaw, tongue, and air flow move when saying the different sounds that make up a word and then with deciding what letters match the sounds and air flow.

Next, even though the spoken word is fluid and smooth, your child needs to decipher and work his writing so that his words have beginning, middle, and ending sounds. These letter clusters must be bounded by spaces.

Your child then must combine this knowledge by mentally storing the sounds and syllable configurations in his mind, along with the configurations of how to represent the written word on paper.

It is only after all of this that your child must retrieve from his memory the stored information and physically reproduce it on paper. He must take in his hand his pencil and form the strings of lines and dashes that make up letters.

Such a difficult and challenging exercise and all done by a beginning writer—pretty amazing, don't you think?

# Reading Ideas and Activities

Reading is a crucial component in any spelling study. Reading allows spellers to see words written in print and in a sequential and organized order. It builds their vocabulary for writing and allows them to manipulate the written and spoken word.

Hence, reading together with your child is of the utmost importance. Your child is still building confidence with written language. They need you there for support and encouragement. They also need you there to toss about ideas and thoughts they have about the language. So be there for them, help them, and encourage them. Let the love of reading grow and prosper from you to them.

Please refer to chapter 1 for reading strategies and ideas. Great reads to introduce at this stage are nursery rhymes, Dr. Seuss, and books with predictable rhyming and repeating patterns.

*Econo-saver:* Remember to use the library to borrow books and always check out book and garage sales for great used books.

# Writing Ideas and Activities

## MODELING

At this stage, it is equally important to have your child write often, preferably every day. When your child is immersed in his writing, sit with him, and talk about what is being written down; help him get his thoughts and stories down on paper. Children need to see that they can create written language. The generalizations that the children discover are meaningful and stay with them.

It is beneficial to engage in a lot of talk about words while you are with your child. Help him to form generalizations about his word writing. Whenever possible, ask questions like: "What do you have to do with writing to make words? What do all words have? What do you notice about the letters?" and so on and so forth.

Constantly build on your child's vocabulary by soliciting risk-taking attempts at naming the beginning and ending sounds in the words. Make it fun and challenging by problem solving and detective work.

To begin this process, create a great and enticing writing center. In chapter 1, there is a great section on what a writing center should look like and what to include in it. Please refer to it. At this stage of writing development, I would also add to the writing center some colorful, fun, and interesting journals, funky pencils and pens, and a personal homemade Student Word Book and dictionary. Refer to chapter 2 on how to make the dictionary and Student Word Book.

## FUN AND GAMES

At this stage, your child is experimenting with letter-to-sound and pattern reproduction in a word-like format. To foster this interest, work with specific games. Let children play with alphabet cards, magnetic letters, and alphabet blocks. One great option is to play Internet games such as Magnetic Word Board. You can also build activities around word families and other word games using alphabet cards. At this age, children love making their own games and activities and are more than capable of doing so. In the following text are several game and activity ideas. Use them, modify them, or create your own. It's worth the experience.

*Econo-saver:* Collect and recycle old birthday, Christmas, and greeting cards. Cut out the backs and use them for all your blank card needs.

*Econo-saver:* Laminate all games and pieces of equipment that you plan to use repeatedly. Copy and mail service stores have laminators. You can always "laminate" your own with clear plastic Mac-tac, available at any large department store.

*Econo-saver:* Organize all games into sturdy baggies and file them in file folders and boxes. Label everything with permanent marker clearly, for easy future access.

### Build-A-Word Games

Following the Scrabble game letter distribution, check the Internet for letter distribution, make several duplicates of the letter tiles. Having lots of letters to work with is time-consuming yet necessary. You can go to any game store and purchase letter tiles, too.

Play simple spelling games with your alphabet cards. Quick, off-the-top-of-my-head game suggestions are: your own version of Scrabble, hangman, Spill and Spell, Boggle, dominoes, word bingo, word finds, crosswords, rummy, Word Lotto, I Spy, Go Fish, concentration, and Tic-Tac-Toe. Use and modify any word matches/word sort games.

### Matching and Concentration Games

To make your own, create a deck of cards from magazines, old calendars, and computer or hand-drawn cuttings of pictures and objects on card stock or index cards. Create picture sets of threes, choosing one topic (initial consonants, blends, digraphs, vowel sounds, word endings; for example). Sort them into a set of two correct and one incorrect word cards (example for the consonant sound of *m*: man, mat, and ham).

To play the game, lay a set of three cards facing up on the table. Have your child choose the correct two, then write out the words to verify answer. More challenging sets can be made as the child's comprehension increases to include initial consonant blends and digraphs and word endings.

Another version of this game can be made and played. As before, make a deck of cards according to a pre-determined topic: initial consonants, blends, digraphs, vowel sounds, word endings, and so on. This time, create a second set of corresponding letter cards to match every picture card.

When ready, shuffle together the decks of matching picture and letter cards (no more than twelve of each) and place face down in neatly organized rows. Players take turns turning over two cards per turn. The player must read the letter card, identify the picture, and state whether it is a match. If the two cards form a match (letter card and picture card), then the person gets to keep his cards. If not, the cards are returned to a face down position and the play moves to the next player. The game continues until all matches are revealed. Players count their cards, and the one with the most wins. My students and two daughters always love to play these type of games. I'm certain yours will, too!

### Word Sort Games

Playing sorting games according to certain sounds and word families is fun and engaging. This can be as simple as cutting pictures from magazines and sorting them according to a related topic, or purchasing commercially prepared games such as Scrabble, Junior Scrabble, Up Words, Boggle, Scattergories, and others.

*Econo-saver:* Have you heard this one before? Garage sales and flea markets are great places to find used games at bargain prices.

*Econo-saver:* Games make great gifts: for birthdays, graduations, holidays or any special occasion. Don't be afraid. Here's the secret: kids love games!

### Hide and Seek Game

To prepare for this game, write a complete sentence using index, card stock, or blank cards, placing one word on each card. Arrange the word cards face up on the floor in correct sentence order. Read the sentence with your child and follow the words by indicating each one with your finger as you both read aloud.

Next tell your child to close his or her eyes tightly. There is no peeking allowed! Now turn over one of the words to hide it and have the child identify the hidden word. Reverse the role and have your child be the "word hider" and you the "word seeker."

You can also use the cards from this game to create another interacting activity. This time, mix up the cards, and spread them randomly on the table. Have your child rearrange the cards in correct, sequential sentence.

### Sound Letter Rummy

This activity can be done during a family night or rainy day get-together. You need: two to four players, fourteen four-card picture sets (fifty-six cards) from magazines, old calendars, or computer or hand-drawn cutouts of pictures and word captions with their initial, ending, or vowel sounds printed on the card.

If more than two people and fewer than five people are playing, shuffle the cards and deal eight cards to each of the four players. Place an extra card face up on the table to start the discard pile, and the remainder of the deck should be also placed face down beside it. In a two-player game, each player is dealt a hand of ten cards, and when five or six play, each player gets six cards.

The first player takes one card from either the top of the face down pile or the top card on the discard pile, and adds it to his hand. Unlike the other "face down" pile, the discard pile consists of cards that are all face up, and everyone can see what is discarded. Once you've chosen a card, you cannot change your mind and return it to the pile. If you draw from the face down pile, you add the card to your hand without showing it to the other players.

At the end of your turn, one card must be withdrawn from your hand and placed on top of the discard pile face up. If you began your turn by picking up the top card of the discard pile, you are not allowed to end that turn by discarding the same card, thus leaving the pile unchanged—you must discard a different card. You may, however, pick up a discarded card on one turn and discard that same card at a later turn. Conversely, if you draw a card from the face down pile, it can be discarded and added to the discard pile on the same turn.

When you have a set of four matching cards with matching sounds (initial, final, word endings, or vowel sounds), you must lay them down. The game continues until all cards are used and, in the process, players are eliminated one by one. The winner is the one holding the most sets of cards.

When you're ready to move onto a more concentrated study of consonant blends and digraphs that would provide your child with even more knowledge regarding sound relationships in writing and spelling, try the following games.

### Word Blend Digraphs—Mix and Match

A mixed, modified version of concentration and dominoes. In preparation for this game, make a deck of twenty-eight standard consonant blends and digraphs playing cards. Search the Internet for consonant blends and digraphs listings.

When finished creating the cards, make a set of thirty-three word family cards (your choice), which is used to form words by adding these to the above consonant blends and digraphs. Search the Internet for examples of standard word families:

Finally, create two wild cards (or blank cards). Add the wild cards to the word family deck. These wild cards are used to make a word when drawn.

The game is simple. The object of the game is to match consonant blend cards with word family cards to make words.

Shuffle each deck of cards separately. The consonant blend deck is handed to your child and the word family deck is placed face down on the table. The child then places eight consonant blend cards in a row, leaving enough space to lay word family cards beside each one. This is followed by your child drawing from the word family pile and placing that card alongside a consonant blend card that together makes a word. The child continues to draw from the word family deck, making words with the consonant blends until all possibilities are played out.

This game can be played with two or more people by dealing out the family word cards evenly among the players. Each person plays until they can no longer play. The play then advances to the next player.

The game continues until all cards are played out. The winner is the first one out or the one with the fewest cards left in her hand.

A modified Spit Card Game can be played with two players. The object is to lay word family cards next to the consonant blend cards in order to form words. The first player to empty her hand is the winner. You can create the same game for word endings using word card sets and word endings card sets to match. A matching rummy game can also be put together where the object of the game is to match the singular nouns with the correct plural nouns. With all word endings, remember to include both regular and irregular nouns.

### Blend Spin Chase

To play the game, you need a pre-made spinner and game board, as well as playing pieces. Search the Internet for spinner masters. Place a blend on each section of the spinner and do not forget to add some miss-a-turn, advance two squares, or go back two spaces sections on the game board. On each space on the game board, draw or paste a picture that begins with the blends you have chosen and placed on the spinner.

When everything is made and gathered, you're ready to start the game. Begin by placing everyone on the start position; determine who goes first (either by birthday, age, highest roll on dice, etc.), and the first player spins. The player reads the blend and advances to the picture that represents the blend shown on the spinner. If the person is correct, he is permitted to stay on the square. If the person chooses the wrong picture, he must return to his last position and forfeits his turn. The next player advances. The game continues until a player reaches the finish line. This game can be modified for digraphs, vowel sounds, word endings, or any other desired focus.

### Word Puzzles

Before you play this game, decide on your area of focus, such as blends and digraphs. Gather the word family cards, and blends and digraphs cards. Shuffle both decks of cards separately. Place the word family deck, face down, in front of your child and spread out the other card deck (the focus of study), face up, around the playing surface.

**Figure 3.3.    Lauren**

After that, have your child draw the first card from the word family deck and then search for consonant blends and digraphs to make words from the deck of cards spread out on the table. Once the player can no longer find words to make with the word family card, it becomes the next player's turn. He now draws from the word family deck. Play continues, with players changing every time a new word family card needs to be drawn, until all words have been exhausted. The winner is the one with the most words, of course.

To make the game more exciting and fast-paced, divide the word family deck into two equal piles and place a pile in front of each of you. Have a race to see who can make the most words within a certain time limit. The winner would be the person with the most made words.

### Word Checkers

You need to borrow, buy, or make a checkerboard and pieces. Paste word families on each square—a different one for each square. Search the Internet for word families. Now you're ready to play Word Checkers. Play the game as you would ordinary checkers, but when you make a move, in order to stay there, you must be able to provide a consonant letter, consonant blend, or digraph to make a word and you must also spell the word correctly. If you are unable to do so, the player must return to his previous square and forfeits his turn. The game continues like a regular game of checkers. My student, Drew, a highly competitive and competent chess player loves this game! He beats me every time!

## Word Baseball

This is a great game to play on a rainy day or family night gatherings. To get ready to run the bases, you need to make a stack of word family cards cut in the shape of baseballs. You also need a baseball diamond game board and playing pieces (colored playing counters or even little stand up soldiers).

Place the baseball word family cards face down on the table with the game board and divide into two teams. Decide who begins the game (oldest, youngest, next birthday, or highest roll on dice).

To play the game, take turns drawing a baseball from the stack. The player reads the family word card, and then adds a consonant letter, consonant blend, or digraph to make a word. He must then spell the word correctly and move his game piece to first base. If the player is unable to create a new word, his team receives an out. The team continues to advance to the bases. Same as in regulation baseball, after three outs, you switch teams. Game continues until all nine innings are played.

Depending on the time, innings may be limited. This game can be played just as easily with only two players. My students loved to play it; they would ask to play it during their free-time.

## Word Bowling

A game of bowling where the players make words to bowl. You need word family bowling cards (that is, word families written on bowling ball shaped cards and numbered from 1–10 on the backside), a word bowling score card (a card with players' names written on it and spaces for recording scores), and a bag.

Divide the players into two teams. Decide who begins the game (oldest, youngest, next birthday, or highest roll on dice). Place the bowling score sheet and a bag of bowling family word cards on a table in front of you. A game, or "string," is made up of ten frames. Each frame represents one turn for the bowler and, in each turn, the player is granted to draw a bowling word family card, twice.

Drawing a bowling ball card from the bag, the player reads the word family card and adds a consonant letter, consonant blend, or digraph to make a word. He must then spell the word correctly. If the word is correct, the player turns over the card to see his score. The score is recorded on the score sheet and a second draw from the bowling word family card bag is given. The same procedure is required with respect to reading, identifying, spelling, and scoring. If any word is incorrect, the player receives no score for a "gutter ball." After two cards are drawn and played, it becomes the next team's play. The game continues passing the turn to a new team member for each rotation, until all ten frames are recorded on the score sheet.

The winning team is the team with the highest score. This game is easily played with two players. I have gotten myself in terrible class disputes as the game "rages" on in the classroom competition and playoffs.


## PENCIL AND PAPER ACTIVITIES

There are many pencil and paper activities that enhance your child's level of word understanding and spelling based on attending to sound and patterns. Remember to include them in your car pocket caddy, when traveling (for details, see chapter 2).

### Letter Fill

Provide the first letter, a specific number of blanks (2 to 3) and the last letter. Let your child make as many words as possible by filling in the blanks, for example, *b _ _ d*: bold, bead, bled, bard, bald, band, bred.

### Mix and Match

Give your child a variety of word family cards, consonant blends, and digraphs cards. Challenge them to make as many words as possible using different combinations. They should then check their ideas for accuracy in a dictionary or word book.

### Pyramid Words

All players draw a pyramid on a sheet of papers, with squares. The first row has one square, the second row two, an so on up to nine. The players enter a word into each row according to the number of squares. The first player to complete her pyramid is the winner.

### New Word Maker

Have kids add or delete letters to form a string of new words starting with a base word you provide to them, for example, *an*: and, hand, band, brand, strand, and so forth. See how long you can make the string.

### Word Mazes

Seek out or create word mazes. At this level, avoid word mazes with words written backwards. Have your child create words mazes to copy for trips.

*Econo-saver*: You can buy word mazes at magazine stores or search the Internet and copy or create your own.

### Words within Words

Challenge students to find all the other words within a specific word, such as, for example, *mother*: moth, other, he, her, the.

### Word Accordion

Take a regular 8½" × 11" sheet of paper, and fold it into five-centimeter sections widthwise, making an accordion with your sheet of paper. One person writes a word on the first fold. By manipulating the letters to make other words, the next person changes one sound in the word and writes a new word on the next paper fold. The paper is continually passed around to the next person until the accordion is filled or no other changes can be made. See what word can make the most new words.

### Whimsical Word Writings

Choose particular consonant letters, consonant blends, ending digraphs, word endings, or vowels and brainstorm with your child words containing those letters. Write the words down and check with a dictionary to verify

**Figure 3.4.    Mom and Lauren**

the words. Have the child underline, circle, or fancy up the beginning consonant letters, blends, final digraphs, or vowel sounds. Emphasize the sounds when saying the words out loud.

### Chain Words

You write one word and your child has to come up with another word that starts with the last letter or ending of your word. Use a dictionary for help. The play continues until all words are exhausted. Make sure you have your child underline, circle, and highlight the beginning consonant letter, blends, word endings, vowels, and so on, and practice saying the word, articulating and stressing the consonant letters, consonant blends, final digraphs, word endings, or vowels.

### Spectacular Sentence Strips

Some specific and engaging activities to encourage word and sentence making are important to explore. Sit with your child and write down familiar sentence strips and matching individual word cards. Have the child select and place in order the words that make up the sentence strip. In the process, make sure to mix up the cards and place them in baggies for future use. For an added challenge, play the Hide and Seek game by hiding a word card and having your child identify the missing word.

## COMMERCIAL WORD GAMES

There are many commercial word games on the market today. Do a quick search on the Internet or visit a game store to browse the selections. Here is a quick list to get you started: Academy of Magic, Acropolis, Babel Delux, Big Kahuna Words, Bonnie's Bookstore, Book Worm Delux, Flip Words, Reader's Digest Super Word Power, Scrabble, Shangri La Delux, Spelvin Delux, Super Letter Linker, Super Twist, Super What Word, Text Express Delux, Wheel of Fortune, Wild Wild Word, Word Cross, Word Harmony, Word Long To Go, Word Monaco, Word Slinger, Word Spiral, and Word Travels.

## INTERNET WEBSITE WORD GAMES

As is the case with commercial games, there are many fun and exciting games to be found on the web. Here are a few examples just to get you started: A Game A Day Interactive, Ask Oxford, Boxerjam Chihuahua Daily Word Puzzle, CR Puzzles, Cryptagram, English Banana, Flipside, Game Desire, Gamer Play, Games 2 Cool, Gopher Gas, Hoadworks, I Win, Kurnik Online Games, Learning Vocabulary Can Be Fun, Letterbox Word Game Online, Miningco.com, Mystery NetPlanet Spogg, Pogo, Puzzability, Quick Words, Rec.puzzles Archive, Remittag, StudyStack, SYZYGY, Thinks.com, Vocabulary University, Weave Words, Word Games For Catholics, Word Games From East Of The Web, Word Safari, Wordox, WordZap, and Yahoo Word Games.

## LISTENING AND RHYMING ACTIVITIES

To develop and increase a child's auditory discrimination of initial and blended sounds, it is best to provide activities that require the child to listen and respond. Begin with a simple activity such as Blend Batch. Arrange one or two picture cards with a beginning sound or blend on a table or another flat surface. Have your child rummage through a picture card collection to find other pictures illustrating words that begin with the same sound or blend.

*Econo-saver:* A quick and inexpensive way of collecting picture cards is using old calendars and magazines. Garage sales are also great places for deals at reasonable prices, as well as year-end sales at calendar shops. Laminate them to preserve them for year after year usage.

When your child is successful at these games and ready to move on, work toward orally presenting two or three words in a group and have your child identify sounds by saying "same" or "different" in accordance to whether the words have the same beginning sound or different. When a child advances, have them search out words with consonant blends, ending digraphs, word endings, and vowel sounds.

You can say several words with the same beginning, ending, or vowel sounds. In this case, have the child look around their environment to pick words from what he sees and match the letter/sound with a word of his choice. Switch positions and play the game again. You can also pair the spoken word with the written word, but remember that some same sounds have different spellings, such as, for example, *kite* and *cat*, and *flower* and *phone*.

Rhyming activities with word families can foster sound distinction, as well as further word meaning and spelling. Begin with reading and rehearsing old favorite nursery rhymes with your child. Read aloud several times. Make the reading and listening fun by using different voices, hand gestures, and facial expressions. Have children sound and clap the rhyming words. As you share/read with them, it is good to pause at the end of phrases and let your child provide the rhyming words. You can even look up words in the dictionary or on the internet.

I remember teaching my children various nursery rhymes. There are so many of them: Going to St. Ives, Five Little Ducks, Old Mother Hubbard, Ring Around the Rosie, Little Miss Muffet, There was a Crooked Man, There was an Old Lady Who Swallowed a Fly, Three Little Kittens, Little Mouse, Peter, Peter, Pumpkin-Eater, and so on. My kids love them, as do I. As you are reciting them, also illustrate the rhyme together with your child.

Once they are familiar with and can recite several rhymes, try playing substitution and close activities with them. Simply have them substitute other rhyming words. Here's an example: "As I was going to St. Ives, I met a man with seven wives (chives, knives, or beehives)." Try playing Thumbs Up; Stand Up, Sit Down; I Spy; Slap and Clap; or I Say You Say.

In Thumbs Up, children put their thumbs up when they hear a pair of rhyming words. Start with a series of pair words, such as *kite* and *snack*, *bird* and *hat*, *fight* and *light*. To add challenge to the game, have your child finish the list with another rhyming word, such as *right*.

In order to inject a little beneficial physical activity, you can change the game to Stand Up, Sit Down. Say a list of rhyming words and remain standing; say a nonrhyming word and you have to sit down.

When playing I Spy, children begin with the phrase: "I spy with my little eye something that rhymes with _____, (a word that sounds like *duck*)." The play partner or the first child with their hand up says (muck, puck, chuck, for example). The game continues until all rhymes are exhausted.

Children love to rhyme and one of the most fun rhyming games they play at recess or during free-time is the Old Snap and Clap Game. Kids play this all the time. My one daughter plays this game while carpooling with her friends to highland dance. To play this game, sit opposite each other (or in a circle with a group) with your legs crossed, then clap twice, snap once. and say a word. Your partner or the next person in the circle has to repeat the two claps, one snap, and end by saying a word that rhymes with the word the previous person said. The game continues until all rhyming words have been exhausted, or all players have been knocked out by pausing or giving or incorrect rhyme. You can make the game more challenging by using more intricate clap and snap routines and more complicated rhyming schemes.

Another option is to try the I Say, You Say Game. For example: "I say hat, you say _____, (a rhyming word for hat)." Play these games using word endings for the theme.

An additional fun and engaging sound-to-letter study is playing tongue twisters. Everyone loves a tongue twister. I recall: "She sells seashells by the seashore," "Peter Piper picked a pack of pickled peppers," and "How much wood would a woodchuck chuck, if a woodchuck could chuck wood?" Read, practice, and recite them. Have lots of fun. Experiment with different voices and add action. Teach these famous tongue twisters to your child, challenging them to a race of saying them as fast as they can without getting mixed-up. That's when the laughter comes into play. There are many tongue twisters one can learn. Search the Internet for ideas.

For visual awareness and spelling of rhyming words, it is good to play any of these games with pencil and paper. Two-word rhymes (echo-word reduplication) are created when two similar words or words which are nearly alike in sound are put together, such as: hodgepodge, nitwit, ding dong, wishy-washy, tick-tock, and so forth. This can be done by changing the vowel as in *pitter-patter* or by changing the initial consonant or consonant cluster as in *willy-nilly*. Brainstorm as many different word rhymes as you can think of and then make up your own.

To engage your child further in this activity, you can make up riddles about your two-word rhymes and see if your child can solve the riddles. For example, "It means to tread with little chatter." The answer is: pitter-patter.

Remember to incorporate tongue twisters too. Once you feel that both your child and you have become experts in reciting tongue twisters orally, try making up your own on paper. This activity helps with visual learning and spelling conventions. You can play this as a twosome, but it's much more fun to play with a group.

Write everyone's full names, including any nicknames the group may have. Choose one of the names to use (names that begin with *b, d, l, m, p, s,* or *t* are easiest) and write it down on a piece of paper. Thereafter, have the person sitting next to you write an answer to "What did she do?" You can use a dictionary. Your answer must begin with the first sound in the person's name (e.g., Mary—made a mess). You then pass the paper again and write an answer for "where," again using the same sound that makes the beginning of the name. Continue this process by answering questions such as "when" or "why" and by continuing sentences with the use of the term "because." Remember to use the same sound that the original chosen name begins with. At the end, you have created a silly tongue twister. Read it aloud to the group and have a great chuckle.

Challenge the group by expanding the answer through the use of more than one word of the same sound/letter. Recognize your child's creative attempts at creating and writing tongue twisters by adorning her work with a beautiful drawing or collage of magazine cut-outs and display it proudly.

These activities and games provide exposure to print and assist in developing within-word pattern knowledge, further allowing children to understand that spoken and written language can be broken down into segments (sounds) represented by letters. Children who are at this stage of spelling development are formulating rules and standards (connections) between the articulation of a word and the way it is written.

Once your child has mastered rhyming words with Nursery Rhymes, two-word rhymes, and tongue twisters, it would be time to introduce good old Dr. Seuss (the master of silly rhymes), and together you can create your very own Big Book of silly rhymes.

As children experiment with language using the letter-to-sound strategy, they are becoming "true" phonetic spellers. As a matter of fact, much of the children's inventive spelling was once considered conventional spelling during the Old English Period. Their spelling is composed of the letters that most clearly represent the sounds they make.

However, many letters occur within words that are not for sound-letter representation, but are for pronunciation cues (i.e., in the word *make*, the *e* does not make a sound, but does indicate to the speller that the *a* is long and a child in this stage would spell *make* as *mak*. Thus, a child's spelling at this stage of development is still nonconventional.

At any time, if something jars your memory and you think it would be interesting and purposeful, use it or modify it for your individual child. Be a risk-taker yourself; be creative and try it out. If it doesn't work for you or your child, then throw it away and move on. Come on, you can do it!

# CHAPTER 4

# Middle Elementary Years

## Spelling Background Knowledge: Polysyllabic and Structural Pattern Concept

Children at this stage of development are conventional spellers. They spell many basic sight and high-frequency words consistently and automatically. As conventional spellers, these children are able to mentally picture letter sequences and structures of words and thus are able to recognize when a word doesn't look right and think of alternative spellings. They know what is right in context—for example, *their*, *there*, and *they're*.

Children as conventional spellers are growing in their writing maturity however. Previously omitted consonant nasal sounds appear in the child's writing as in *limp* instead of *lip*, and *sunk* instead of *suk*. The use of long and short vowels as pronunciation cues are materializing. The choice may still be incorrect, as the word *name* may be spelled *naem*, and the word *feed* may be spelled *fede*. Word endings are generally correct, though children may experience difficulty with double consonant endings. They may spell *supper* as *super* and similarly, *hoping* as *hopping*. The routine use of *r*-controlled syllables is more apparent, even though it is not heard or felt as a separate sound. The choice of vowel representation may still be incorrect as in the spelling of *monstur* for *monster*.

As children work through this stage, they learn to differentiate between different spellings of the same sound, like the *oi* sound found in the words *oil* and *boy*. They begin to use and understand that words may be categorized into phonograms (also known as word families), which are predictable patterns or "chunks" within words such as the *ate* family: bake, skate, and fate. Children learn that similar sounds are represented by several different letters or groups of letters. Such as the long *e* sound found in the words: even, chief, eat, tree, happy, monkey, and me; the *z* sound found in the words: present, applause, and gauze. They understand that different sounds can be represented by the same letter or string of letters. As in the *ch* digraph found in the words: character, chorus, chauffeur, chute, choir, chimp and chain (which have four different sounds).

Children at this level of spelling development are also venturing with and attempting to understand syllables and their place in spelling. These children are beginning to use more words with more than one syllable, and the spelling and pronunciation cues become significantly more important for their standard writing. Children can no longer rely on sound-to-letter spelling. Spelling becomes more sophisticated and intricate.

I wanted to include a description and an understanding of the vowel sound *schwa*. I've placed it here in this chapter rather than in previous chapters because even though it is a vowel, it does not arise as an error in spelling until multi-syllable words are used.

It is a crucial vowel to study when spelling for two reasons. First, it is the most common vowel in the English language and, secondly, it is a very difficult vowel for children to identify and distinguish. It is commonly misrepresented or omitted.

The vowel sound *schwa* is a neutral vowel that is neither long nor short and is found in an unstressed or non-accented syllable. It is therefore found in words with more than one syllable. Generally, in words with more than two syllables, the *schwa* vowel is located in the middle syllable, although not always, as in the case of the word *decimal*—the *i* and the *a* are both *schwa* vowels occurring in the middle and last syllable. For the most part, the *schwa* vowel sound in a two-syllable word is identified by the "*uh*" pronunciation and sound.

Oftentimes, children spell *chocolate* as *choclat*, *separate* as *seprate*, *vegetable* as *vegtable* or *memory* as *memry*. The *schwa* vowel is thus omitted. The vowel sound *schwa* is also found in two-syllable words, such as alone, pencil, syringe, and taken. Children commonly misrepresent the *schwa* vowel and spell these words: *ulone* for *alone*, *pencol* for *pencil*, *suringe* for *syringe*, and *takin* for *taken*. It is still the vowel in the unstressed syllable that is featured in this case; although the vowel is not omitted. This time, it is substituted with another incorrect vowel.

These aforementioned misunderstandings generally disappear as the child advances in his reasoning and knowledge of the English language, learns conventional alternatives for representing sounds, and begins to apply patterning including syllables and a visual sense to his spelling.

Trevor's writing uses many standard spellings (sees figure 4.1a and b). His printing is clear and legible. Trevor is using punctuation and paragraphing. He is aware that syllables have vowels, as is reflected in his

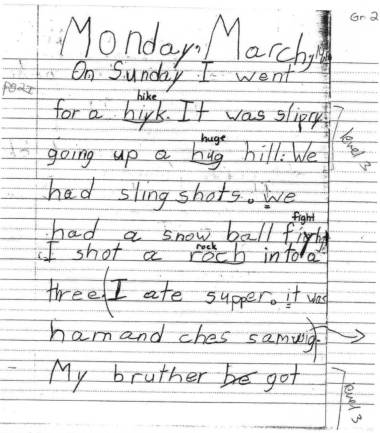

**Figure 4.1a.    Trevor's writing sample**

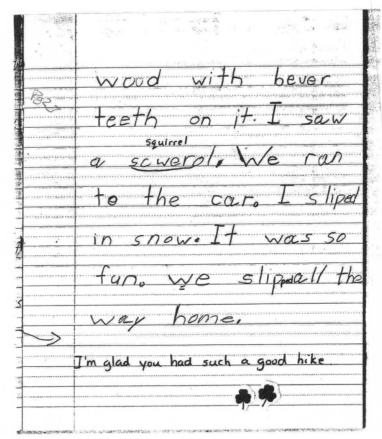

wood with bever
teeth on it. I saw
a *squirrel*
scwerol. We ran
to the car. I sliped
in snow. It was so
fun. we slipedall the
way home,

I'm glad you had such a good hike.

**Figure 4.1b.**

spelling of *beaver*—*be•ver* and *squirrel*—*scwer•ol*. Trevor is also attempting to use long-vowel pronunciation cues, but still is not versed in the correct ones. He has spelled *hiyk* for *hike*, *fiyht* for *fight* and *bever* for *beaver*. The spelling of *slipry* for *slippery*, without the vowel in the unstressed middle syllable, is a common *schwa* vowel omission. Additionally, Trevor's understanding of doubling letters before endings is still immature as he has spelled *slipped* as *sliped* and *slippery* as *slipry*.

Christine is a lovely story teller. Her writing is very personal (see figure 4.2). Christine's printing is neat, organized, and well spaced.

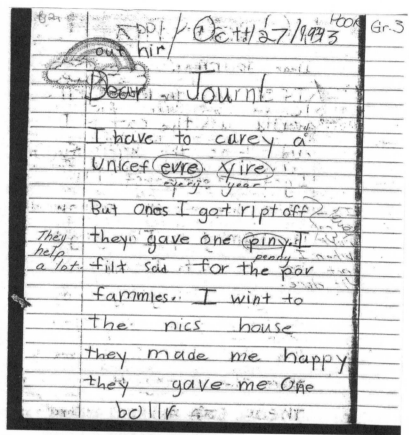

**Figure 4.2.   Christine's writing sample**

She is aware of vowel usage in her writing; however, she still encounters difficulty with short and long vowels. Her short vowel sounds are sometimes incorrect, as is shown in her writing of *filt* for *felt*; *piny* for *penny*, and *wint* for *went*. Christine understands the role long vowels play in spelling and pronunciation, though she uses incorrect long vowel strategies as with *evre* for *every*, and *yire* for *year*. I am surprised to see her write *por* for *poor*. I think she is using the letters *o* and *r* as the "or" in her writing of "poor."

Christine is advanced in that she appears aware of syllables and how each syllable must have a vowel, as in *carey* for *carry* and *fammles* for *families.* She is attempting to include word endings in her spelling. Her choices in this case remain incorrect, as is shown in *ript* for *ripped* and, again, in *fammles* for *families.* Christine also has difficulty with the *schwa* vowel sound, as in her use of *dollr* instead of *dollar.*

## READING IDEAS AND ACTIVITIES

If as the old saying by Thomas Carlyle goes, "A good book is the purest essence of a human soul," then reading is the emotional adventure. Enjoy the trip. The study of books on syllables is engaging and certain to get the mind focused and flowing. Talk to your local librarian or teacher, and search the Internet for referrals. Look for stories with rhyming and repeating patterns. Good old Nursery Rhymes and repetitive word-picture books are essential. We are never too old to revisit them. In addition, check out music and song books looking for syllabic patterning. Always, always take the time to read aloud; we are never too old. Share the love and excitement of the written and spoken word.

## WRITING IDEAS AND ACTIVITIES

As children progress and experiment with language, their spelling matures to include the understanding and need for the study of patterns. Syllabification, the dividing of a word into units of spoken language that is more than a speech sound and is made up of one or more vowel sounds, is the most commonly noticeable and primary word pattern to study. When given the opportunity and chance for exploration, children attempt to group letters according to the number of syllables that they hear.

At this level of spelling development, children need to learn that when spelling a word, there are regularly more letters in the word than there are syllables. They need to practice, mentally holding onto and manipulating sounds and syllables in words and to learn when, where, and how to use vowels and syllables as pronunciation cues, which is the basic process in sounding out (phonemic segmentation).

Learning to use these patterns involves classifying and sorting words by these patterns and actively noting the similarities and differences by sight, sound, and touch. I bet that when you, as an adult, learn to spell a new word, you don't sit down and write out the new word ten times, memorize it by rote, and then spell it correctly time and again in different written assignments. I bet that instead, you would look at the pattern, make connections to other spellings you are familiar with, use it in your writing, and make a conscious effort to remember it. This process, tried and true, should be no different for children. What do you think? Give the kids the secrets.

Learning happens when you connect new spellings with what you already know and use. The most valuable way to study words and patterns is within the children's own writing. This way motivation and success are ensured and the level of spelling is appropriate. Furthermore, talking with children about their own personal writing further reinforces their hypotheses, observations, and discoveries.


## VISUAL SYLLABIC WORK

Using a hand-held mirror, have your child explore facial movements as they practice saying polysyllabic words. Talk about how the facial parts feel when different movements are applied. Talk about how the lips pucker when saying *pink*, are wide open when saying *apple*, or are stretched wide apart when saying *whistle*.

Observe how the teeth rest on the lower lip when saying *love*; how the tongue sits on the ridge behind the teeth on the upper side of the mouth when saying *dragon*; pushes in between the upper and lower teeth when saying *think*; touches the roof of the mouth when saying *church*; or hits the back of the mouth when saying *kick*, and also how the sound comes from opening the back of your throat when saying *house*.

Have your child place his hands on the moving parts of his face and throat, and have him feel the movement and vibrations. Have him focus at looking at and feeling the movements. Allow your child the opportunity to see himself in the mirror. Some children may feel awkward when looking at themselves. Others love to make silly expressions and watch themselves in the mirror.

Once they are quite comfortable with using the mirror and describing their observations, have them watch and count the times their mouth opens and closes, as well as the number of times their jaw drops when saying polysyllabic words. Do this several times with a list of polysyllabic

**Figure 4.3.    Graeme and Jessica**

words. Have them watch your mouth movements and count the times your own mouth opens and closes and your jaw drops.

*Econo-saver:* You can purchase inexpensive hand-held mirrors at the dollar store or even metallic posterboard at craft stores.

You can always videotape your child or yourself while demonstrating or experimenting with polysyllabic words. You can use a video recorder or even a digital camera. View the recording or pictures together while discussing and pointing out highlights. The nice thing about viewing a recording is that you can pause the recording at any time.

## KINESTHETIC SYLLABIC WORK

When teaching children a new concept, it is imperative to teach and explore many different methods and applications. The more strategies that are applied and exposure to methods gained, the higher the success and understanding.

Have your child practice placing her hands on your jaw and feel your facial movements. Have her describe in words what she is feeling and noticing. She can also practice on her brother, sister, or grandpa—anyone willing to lend a jaw. Do this several times and watch out for the occasional outburst of laughter. When a child becomes an expert examiner and communicator, have her feel and watch your jaw, as well as count how many times your jaw drops when saying a polysyllabic word. Through practice, she can keep honing her skills until she is confident in counting syllables in words.

Next, have your child clap for each syllable in the spoken word. Say the word naturally and then speak it, emphasizing the syllabic segmentation as your child claps once for each syllable, such as: *teacher—teach • er* (with two claps) and *telephone—tel • e • phone* (with three claps). Have your child clap every syllable he hears in the word you have spoken. Don't get too carried away with the large polysyllabic words. Have your child say a polysyllabic word for you to repeat and tap out on your child's back. Take turns changing roles and repeating the process. Snapping out the syllables is fun, so how about clicking the syllables with your tongue? Practice using touch in as many ways as possible. You can try doing this in so many ways. Be creative.

## AUDITORY SYLLABIC WORK

Once your child is able to distinguish syllables using visual and kinesthetic cues, introduce dividing polysyllabic words orally. Using the same method as described before, say the word naturally and then speak it, emphasizing the syllabic segmentation. Have your child listen to you and count in his head the number of syllables he hears. You can practice this many times, while each sharing both roles as listener and presenter. In no time, your child is distinguishing the syllable segmentation in most words.

As a culminating activity, with all syllable work, it is beneficial to have your child look at several words in syllabic form, as well as analyze and make observations and predictions about the patterns. For example, indicate that a vowel is in every clap or that it is the vowel that causes the mouth to open when saying the word aloud. I've always been astonished with my students when I asked them to make discoveries, patterns, and "aha's"; their finds are always interesting and complex. Similarly, you can help your child make these discoveries and test out her theories. In the process, remember to review and identify the vowel sound heard in each syllable.

Be creative, innovative, and simple. For instance, how about recording your observations on poster board? To do this, make a large table chart on a poster board. Design it as you wish. Include a title, columns (indicating number of syllables in the word), and rows (indicating method of identifying syllables like taps, snaps, and claps) with headings for each. Use your own calligraphy or use design fonts from the computer. Have fun with it. For durability and future usage, laminate the poster board.

Fill in the rest of the cells with words you found together in your child's reading that match the number of syllables and criteria. Above all, have fun learning. Display your work or keep it in a file for future reference.

## SYLLABLE SPELLING PATTERNS

There are six commonly known syllable spelling patterns. Once the child is confident and has mastered the concept of syllabication, begin to study and learn each of the following six syllable spelling patterns: closed, open, r–controlled, double vowels, vowel-silent e, and consonant-le.

Closed syllables end in a consonant, and the vowel is generally short. They follow a vowel-consonant (vc) such as: in, at, it, on; a consonant-vowel-consonant (cvc) such as: cat, hot, met; or a consonant-vowel-consonant-consonant pattern (cvcc) such as: rabbit and napkin.

Open syllables end in a vowel sound and are generally long. They follow the vowel (v) such as *a* or *i*; the consonant-vowel (cv) such as in he, go, *va ca tion*, *mu sic*; and consonant-consonant-vowel (ccv) patterns such as in she, bright, and *pro ba tion*.

R-controlled syllables exist when a vowel is followed by an *r* in the same syllable, making that vowel *r*-controlled. It is neither long nor short. The *r*-controlled syllables *er*, *ir*, and *ur* sound the same. For example: term, sir, fir, fur, far, sugar, and order—all contain an R-controlled syllable. They are identified when a vowel is followed by the letter *r* and the letter affects the sound of the vowel. The vowel and the *r* appear in the same syllable: bird, turtle, and monster.

Vowel teams are *ai*, *ay*, *ea*, *ee*, *oa*, *oo*, *oi*, *oy*, *ou*, *ie*, and *ei*. Double vowels appear in the same syllable as in boat and explain. Be careful of and study all *ea* double vowel combinations. This vowel team can represent three different sounds: the long *e* sound as in *seat*, the short *e* sound as in *death*, and the long *a* sounds as in the word *great*.

The vowel-silent *e* syllable generally represents long-vowel sounds and has a vowel, consonant, silent *e* pattern: compete, decide, and smile. The silent *e* at the end of the word makes the vowel preceding the consonant long and thus say its own name.

The consonant-*le* syllable appears at the end of a word and forms the final syllable. The vowel *e* is silent. The consonant and the *le* combination cannot be segmented into two separate syllables. This is crucial to note when spelling. One must listen to the vowel which comes immediately before the consonant-*le* combination.

If the vowel sound is short and there is another consonant before the consonant-*le* combination, as in the word *single*, there is no problem. The word is divided before the consonant-*le* and what is left, *sin*, is a closed syllable with a short vowel.

However, if this vowel is short and there is no consonant before the consonant-*le* combination, as in *paddle*, then the consonant in the consonant-*le* combination must be doubled. The *d* in *paddle* has to be doubled to close the syllable, thus keeping the vowel sound short. If the *d* were not doubled, the word would still have to have two syllables, *pa-dle*, and the first syllable would be an open syllable in which the *a* would have to say its name and be long. These common syllable-spelling patterns provide students with insight into how words are put together.


## MODELING

When studying these syllable-spelling patterns, it is best to use the "model, think aloud, and choral" routine. Begin by writing a polysyllabic word on paper. Do not say the word out loud. Pause and give your child a chance to study the word.

After a time, model breaking the word into its syllable-spelling pattern. Say out loud what you're thinking while breaking the word into its syllable–spelling patterns. For example: say out loud something like this, "Yes, I know that every syllable must have one vowel sound. In the word *contact*, I see two vowels separated by two consonants. If I divide the word between the consonants, I get *con* and *tact*. Both of these syllables use the closed syllable-spelling pattern since each ends in a consonant. Therefore, I will try the short-vowel sound when pronouncing each syllable: *con-tact*. When I say these two syllables together fluently, I get *contact*." Now think: is *contact* a word that I've heard before, and does it make sense when reading the word in context (the sentence)?

For choral practice, write the words down on paper and, together with your child in chorus, say the words, stressing their syllables. Help your child when necessary.

Through this organized, focused attention and study on common syllable patterns, your child is able to read and figure out longer and more complicated words. Moving into spelling for a purpose, choose purposeful writing experiences. What better place than home to do so? Encourage purposeful writing, such as the writing of messages, lists, plans, signs, letters, stories, songs, and poems.

Both my daughters love making their own personal greeting cards for special occasions and, today, with all the great materials available on the market for scrapbooking, my youngest daughter loves to make mini-scrapbooks filled with her stories, poems, and letters. The recipients of these mini-books are just so thrilled and amazed at the work and thoughtfulness involved.

Frequent application of spelling knowledge by your child while writing, encourages spelling competency. With that in mind, remember to avoid overemphasis on absolute correctness, mechanics, and memorization. Early emphasis on mechanical aspects of spelling inhibits developmental growth and risk-taking. Correctness is nurtured more effectively through knowing where your child is and working from that point, thanks to which you make discoveries together. Remember and constantly remind yourself that complete or perfect understanding and correctedness doesn't always, nor only occur the first time around.

## FUN AND GAMES

### Syllable Sort Activity

This activity can be done with two or more players. Make a T-chart with the names of all syllable patterns as headings, after which you select several words from each syllable pattern. Print them onto card stock and cut them out into cards. Shuffle the cards and distribute them evenly among the players. Each person takes a turn at identifying the syllable type shown on his or her card, placing the card in its appropriate syllable pattern heading, identifying the vowel sound in the syllable, reading the word, and using it in a sentence.

*Econo-saver:* You can handwrite your words on the cards, or you can print them off the computer and glue them onto your card stock. The use of printer labels is quick, easy, and neat.

*Econo-saver:* You can purchase inexpensive card stock at any dollar store.

### Search and Rescue Syllable Hunt

Give your child a piece of paper folded into six columns, and number them one to six. These numbers represent the number of syllables in a word. Have your child select a paragraph from her personal reading, which you use to hunt for words with different numbers of syllables and fill those words in the appropriate columns according to syllable count. The same search and rescue format can be played, using all the six syllable-pattern spellings simply by replacing syllable numbers with the six different syllable patterns. Words are searched, sorted, and placed according to the six syllable-spelling patterns.

### Syllable Battleship Concentration

Create a concentration game board grid master 7 × 7, using square-inch measurements for each cell. The captain (the game monitor) writes on twenty of the game board cells with ten multiple syllable words and ten matching syllable patterns, randomly. Every cell of the game board is then covered with non-see-through markers (pop bottle lids, bingo chips, milk jug caps, whatever), so the players can't see the words and syllables. Players take turns calling out two pairs of coordinates to locate a matching word and syllable pattern. If there is a match the person gets a point, the markers are removed and the next person gets a turn. There is no continuation of play by the person regardless of a win. If the coordinate pairs do not make a match, the person does not get a point; the markers are replaced, and it is the next person's turn to play. The game continues until all words and matching syllable patterns are revealed. The person with the highest score wins.

*Econo-saver:* To make this game reusable, take the game board grid master to a copy place and have them laminate it. While there, you can take the opportunity to purchase dry-erase markers.

### Twenty Questions

Play Twenty Questions with your child. It is a fun activity. To play this game, think of a syllable pattern and word that follows the pattern. Have your child ask yes/no questions regarding your word and pattern. They cannot use any of the syllable spelling pattern words in their questions. All you can answer is: "yes" or "no." If after twenty questions, your child has not come up with the syllable spelling pattern or the word, then you must reveal it.

### Snap

This game is played with two players. Make two decks of twenty-four blank cards from card stock or index cards. Write matching words (in pairs) that represent each of the six common syllable spelling patterns, along with their identification. Keep the two decks separate. Each player is given a set of shuffled cards, and each places the deck face down in front of him or her. At the same time, both players turn over their top card and place it down in front of them. When two cards match according to their identification, the first player to say "snap" wins the pile of cards. The game continues until all cards are matched. The winner is the one with the most cards.

### Beat The Clock

Make two decks of blank cards from card stock. On each card, place a syllable pattern. Do this twice, then shuffle the cards and lay them face down. Turn a card over and set the minute timer. Players write as many words (which follow the syllable pattern) as they can come up with in a minute. Correct syllable patterns are counted and recorded; one point per word. The next round is played. Rounds continue until somebody reaches a hundred. That person is the winner.

*Econo-saver*: Garage sales are great places to find a funky collection of timers. My children and husband love to frequent them.

### The Mad Hatter Game

Pre-write individual questions on strips of paper, for example: name one-syllable nouns, two-syllable verbs, or three-syllable adjectives. When naming verbs, ask for present tense only; it just makes it less complicated.

Then place the strips of questions inside the hat and have your egg timer ready. Draw a question, start the timer, and have everyone race to write as many answers as possible; when the egg timer stops, so do all the players.

The person with the most correct answers is the winner of the hand. Determine in advance to what number you'll race to. Repeat hands again until a person reaches the pre-determined number. The winner of the game is thus declared.

Once your child is comfortable with this game, he is ready to move on. Challenge him by substituting the earlier questions with questions from all six-syllable patterns of spelling. Go for it! Don't be shy.

### *Jelly Bean Toss*

This is a listening game that helps prepare your child for differentiating syllables in words. Prior to the game, make some flash cards. Place a picture of an object on the cards and write the word underneath each picture. Write the answer on the backside of the flash card, with the word broken into its syllables, as well as the number of syllables. Placing the answer in writing allows the child to play by himself, or he can choose to play with others.

When the cards are ready, your child can shuffle the deck and place the cards face own. When a card is drawn, your child sees the picture and reads the word aloud. They listen for the chunks of sounds in the word. Every time they hear a sound chunk, they place a jelly bean inside the box, representing the number of syllables.

For verification, the flash card can be turned over and the jelly beans counted. If correct, the person keeps the jelly beans; if incorrect, the person has to return them. Using Smarties is yummy, too! That is, if you like chocolate. And honestly, who doesn't? My students loved having this game in their spelling centers. Who wouldn't?

### *Jeopardy! A Modified Version*

Jeopardy is a game of trivia covering many topics. It requires at least two contestants, a reader, a game board, questions and answers, a timer, and enough bells per contestant.

The first thing you need to do is to create a game board, six columns by six rows. In the first row of each column, write the subjects of study (i.e., *r*-controlled syllables, vowel-silent *e* syllables, and so on) as headlines.

Then, in each consecutive row and cell, write point values. These could be: the cells in the second row get a point value of one, the cells in the third row get two, and so forth, and so forth.

After the game board is completed, prepare at least thirty-six questions and answers to match the categories of study and their point value.

To play the game, the first contestant (pre-determined by a draw, earliest birth date, number closest to an agreed upon numerical value, and such) selects a category and point value from the game board; then the "reader" selects the corresponding answer, reads it aloud and starts the timer. The contestant to first ring his or her bell must guess the question and ask it aloud.

If the correct question is provided, the contestant receives the point value and is permitted to choose the next category and point value. If he is incorrect or runs out of time, the point value is deducted from his score and any opponent can ring his or her bell and respond. If, at any time, all contestants respond incorrectly or the time runs out, the reader must provide the question. It is then that the person who last provided the correct question gets a turn to choose the next category and point value.

When all cells in the game board have been chosen, the person with the highest score is the winner. That person is the Jeopardy champion.

If you wish to make the game more competitive and longer, you can introduce "daily doubles" in a second round. Re-fill the game board with new category headings. This round, the reader hides three daily doubles in the game board. Only the contestant who selects a Daily Double may respond. The player then selects any point value in any category. If she responds correctly, she gets the daily double (double the point value); if she responds incorrectly, she loses that amount. The game continues until the round ends—that is, when all cells have been chosen. The winner is the person with the highest score.

The use of instructional games enhances your child's growing awareness of words and how they are spelled. Syllable Factory Game, CVC Maker, Count The Syllables, Vowel Boot Camp, and Jeopardy! are just a few options one may find on the Internet. Just search for "syllable Internet games" and browse. Additionally, many commercial games can be purchased and collected, and they make great presents and gifts.

*Econo-saver:* Again, superb places to find inexpensive games are flea markets and garage sales.

## ROAD TRIPS

To face the eternal "Are we there yet?" and "When are we going home?" you should make sure to bring along a good read with you on your trip. Nursery Rhymes and Poetry books are great options. The rhyming patterns focus on syllable counting. Prior to leaving the house, search the Internet, locate, and print out several crosswords, word scrambles, and word searches using rhyming patterns and syllabic terminology. There are some great activities to bring and play while waiting for the time to pass. Here are a few possibilities:

### Making Faces

In order to play this game, you need to procure a hand-held mirror and some Nursery Rhymes. As you read, have your child echo what you say while he is looking in the mirror. Have him watch his jaw and count the drops, telling you how many syllables are to be found in a particular line or verse. After several stanzas, there should be a noticeable pattern occurring.

### Virtual TV

All you need is a good imagination and a dictionary. Open the dictionary to any place. Choose a polysyllabic word. Put on your imagination hat and pretend you are watching television. Look at the picture you see in your mind, then "turn off" the television. Visualize the blackness. Now, put a word on the screen and break it into its syllables. Notice what color marker was used. See what font was used. Notice each syllabic segment. Spell the segments out loud. Finally, write the word down and verify the spelling by using the dictionary.

### Syllable Diction

Using the dictionary, choose a polysyllabic word and read it aloud in its syllabic pronunciation. Have your child echo the word back to you. Have him count the syllables. Using a white board and dry-erase marker, write the word in its polysyllabic segmentation and check with the dictionary for verification. This can be done with stanzas in poetry for an added challenge.

## Skipping

Gather up copies of old favorite skipping songs. Practice learning and singing the songs, as well as rehearsing polysyllabic counting. During travel stops and waiting periods—while practicing with the syllables and moving toward understanding the patterns and rhymes—try substituting your own words and personal stories to change the skipping songs. Write them down in a travel journal.

## Ad Lib Poetry

Using your favorite Nursery Rhymes, copy down verses, but in the second and subsequent lines, leave blanks for the nouns and verbs. Ask your child to replace the parts of speech represented by those blanks. Don't let him see the poem. Make sure the rhyming lines in the stanzas are replaced with rhyming words. For example:

> Hickory Dickory Dock
> Hickory dickory dock
> The (*Noun*) ran up the (Noun that rhymes with dock)
> The clock struck one
> The mouse (*Verb*) down
> Hickory dickory dock

## Ballad Poetry

Ballads are narrative poems that tell a story. They are repeatedly used in songs and have a musical rhythm.

The basic ballad form generally has four-line verses. The second and fourth lines rhyme, following an *abcb* rhythm pattern: *a* stands for one line ending, *b* for another, and *c* for yet another. As a result of the fact that there are two *b*'s, these are the two lines that rhyme. The meter (beats or rhythm) in a basic ballad follows the following pattern per stanza: four stressed syllables, three stressed syllables, four stressed syllables, and three stressed syllables.

Keep in mind that this is a standard, not a must. Ballad writing is not an exact science. The important thing is that your ballad should have a smooth, song-like quality when you speak it aloud. Here is an example:

Have you heard this story,
Of a lad from the prairie sea?
Yearning and searching,
For his lost and lonely laddie.

## Haiku Poetry

Haiku is an unrhymed poem originating from Japan. It captures the essence of a moment keenly perceived and speaks about nature, painting a mental image. The rhythm focuses on syllabic patterning. It mostly includes a three-line, 5-7-5-syllable pattern. For example:

An old croaky frog
Jumped from a green lily pad
Into a dark pool

Your child needs to be encouraged to explore, make connections, and practice with syllabic patterning. These activities help foster a solid understanding of what a word is, as well as provide insight into its structure. When children start to experiment with syllabic patterning, they require a lot of encouragement, as this is a risky thing for them to do. They need lots of time to practice and need to be given permission to make connections and have the understanding that it is okay to make many mistakes within their learning. As adults, we must try to support this practice. Allowing children to learn to spell at their own pace, in a natural, developmental way that is meaningful to them is critical and essential.

# CHAPTER 5

# Upper Elementary Years

## Spelling Background Knowledge: Meaning/Relationships Spelling Concept

Generally, during the middle elementary years and upwards, children can read unknown words with increasing accuracy. They have a solid concept of word structure and basic spelling patterns. Children are able to use visual cues and are able to tell if a word does not look right. Moreover, they have a large selection of memorized and learned spellings.

Errors in writing at this stage of spelling development such as vowel symbol and word endings, regular and irregular plurals, and past tenses are less frequent, as are doubling errors with long and short vowel words. Common English spelling patterns are used more frequently, though perhaps incorrectly: for example, *younited* instead of *united* and *stingks* instead of *stinks*. The same is true for inflectional endings, such as *s*, *'s*, *ing*, and *est*; for example, *bakeing* instead of *baking*, *funnyest* for *funniest*, and *familys* instead of *families* are common spelling errors.

Children at this spelling developmental level are not yet using their spelling principles consistently or automatically due to their sheer lack of experience and writing exposure. As they progress and advance in their learning of spelling, children come to realize that spelling/pronunciation relationships within the context of their reading, phonics, word patterns, predictions, and context are all important components to learning and using correct spelling.

Mastery of spelling now becomes a more complex mental activity that requires cognitive thinking skills: problem solving, memory retention, and mental imagery. Their vocabulary is worldlier and more complicated, thus an understanding and study of etymology; word meaning, origin, and pattern are now necessary and take precedence over sound-to-letter correspondence. On account of this commanding transition from sound-to-letter spelling to meaning within the context of writing, new and more sophisticated spelling errors begin to emerge, often giving the illusion of spelling regression.

Children's spelling vocabulary increases and becomes accurate as they begin to experiment and enjoy learning about word origins and formations, as well as start playing with words. They have fun learning about their meanings and want to use them in their writing when their curiosity is stirred.

Children at this stage of spelling development begin to make critical word formation connections using word meaning and origin through the study and investigation of words. The study of affixes, word patterns, word origins, homonyms, contractions, compound words, word neologisms, and so on are all important activities to incorporate. Word study can be sorted into two categories: form-based and meaning-based word study. Form-based word study includes affixes, homonyms, compound words, and so on, where the study is focused on the patterns, appearances, and configurations of the words. Meaning-based word studies include word relationships comprised of synonyms, themes, and units, where the focus of study is meaning and composition.

Word study is important in the spelling process as it provides the speller with predictable patterning, letter sequencing, and meaning, thus instilling greater confidence and sense of success when the child is "guessing" a spelling word.

Carley's writing is informative and interesting (see figure 5.1). I love how she uses wonderful descriptive words in her writing. Her spelling conventions are good as well. From examining her work, we can determine that she needs to focus on studying homonyms: *there, their,* and *they're,* as well as words such as *it's* and *its.*

Stuart's story is quite different from Carley's (see figure 5.2). His story is written in a diary form from the main character's perspective: a high-level writing skill. Stuart is taking risks in his writing and is giving attention to content and interest over the mechanics of spelling conventions, as is reflected in: *bessnise* and *langweg.* During the editing process of his story, these errors

I think Turtles are the most beautiful creatures in the world. I Love to watch them roam around there little territories. There are lots of different kinds of turtles soft back, hard shell and many more. My personal favorite it is Tortise. With it's short stubby legs, it's long thin neck, it's hard shell with a million and one desinghs on it. All of these things get put tougether to make a Tortise. Its my favorite kind of ----------

Turtle!

Grade 5

**Figure 5.1.    Carley's writing sample**

need to be addressed. It is very beneficial for Stuart to study synonyms such as *grate* and *great*, homonyms such as *there*, *their*, and *they're*, word endings such as *ed*, *ing*, and the correct use of *more* versus *er* endings.

## FORM-BASED WORD STUDY

Affixes, the creation of new words by adding to the original root word (a unit of meaning within a word), are important to investigate, understand, and manipulate. Affixes may be derivational such as *ness* and *pre*, or inflectional such as the plural *s* and past tense *ed*.

Derivational is a word formation process whereby the new word is derived from another existing word by adding affixes and changing its part of speech; for example:

- adjective-to-noun, as in: close—closeness
- adjective-to-verb, as in: visual—visualize

**Figure 5.2.** **Stuart's writing sample**

- noun-to-adjective, as in: joy—joyous
- noun-to-verb, as in: beauty—beautify
- verb-to-adjective, as in: defend—defendable
- verb-to-noun, as in: occur—occurrence

Derivation may also occur without any change of form. For example, in the words *medical* and *medicine*, the *c* in both words sound different; one is a hard *c* and the other is a soft *c*. When children understand that two words are derivative of each other, they can think back, make the connection and are able to "come-up" with the correct spelling.

Inflectional is the modification or changing of a word to indicate grammatical information, such as gender, as in the case of: *actor—actress*, the verb tenses such as: *hand—handed, think—thought, write—wrote—*

*written* , and *sing—sang—sung—singing,* noun plurals such as: *ring—rings* and *boy—boys,* irregular plurals such as: *child—children, mouse—mice* and *foot—feet,* adjectives such as: *tall—taller* and *happy—happiest;* or first person such as *I* or *me,* second person such as *you,* and third person such as *he, him, his, she, her, they, it,* and so on.

Again, when children explore, learn, and understand that words are created by adding inflections and that these inflections affect the grammar and spelling in writing, they are able to retrieve, by looking at the base word, the correct spelling and grammatical placement. Affixes are categorized into several classifications, according to where they are added with reference to the root word. The common English affixes are:

- Prefixes—before the root word (they mostly come from Latin): attend, exit, redo, and unhappy
- Suffixes—after the root: government, condemnation, useless, friendship, telephone, and quickly
- Infixes—within the root word: sang, song, and sing. It is only the vowel that is changing. Other infixes are common in slang words/language such as hip-hop slang. Examples include: *hizouse* or *hizzy* for *house, crizib* for *crib,* and *driz* for *drink;* words created from the TV show "The Simpsons" such as *sophistimacated, saxomaphone,* and *edumacation;* language games such as "pig Latin" and some technical terminology.
- Circumfixes—before and after root word: evaporate, enlighten, and embolden
- Suprafixes—a kind of affix in which the pronunciation, meaning, or parts of speech (the noun and related verb) of a word changes by changing the accent or stressed syllable. Examples include: 'produce (noun) and pro'duce (verb), 'discount (noun) and dis'count (verb), and 'object (noun) and ob'ject (verb).
- Simulfixes—a type of affix that changes one or more existing phonemes (the smallest unit of sound) in order to modify and change the meaning of a morpheme (the smallest meaningful unit in the grammar of a language). Examples of simulfixes in English are generally considered irregularities from singular to plural form such as: mouse—mice, man—men, louse—lice, tooth—teeth, and woman—women, and so forth.

Root words, with their affixes, can combine to create thousands of words. Children gain the knowledge that words often have related words in common and that those words are similar in spelling and meaning even if the pronunciation changes. A similar but reverse process can be applied when spelling words with silent consonants, for example: the *b* in *bomb* to *bombard*, the *n* in *govern* to *government*, and the *g* in *sign* and *signal*. These words with silent letters are heard when we think of their word extensions.

When learning about and working with affixes, one should look for the patterns (i.e., vowel changes). There are three basic vowel patterns/changes that occur: the long vowel to short vowel changes found in words such as *sane* to *sanity, divine* to *divinity,* and *produce* to *production*; the short vowel to *schwa* vowel changes found in words such as *local* to *locality, metal* to *metallic,* and *image* to *imagine*; and the long vowel to *schwa* vowel changes found in words such as *define* to *definition, compete* to *competition,* and *reside* to *residence.* Again, researching, analyzing, and presenting word patterns are all critical steps at this stage of spelling development.

A homonym consists of a group of words that sound the same but differ in spelling, meaning, or origin. Homonyms include the following:

- Homography consists of words with the same spelling though have different meanings, as in the case of *fair* (good or pleasant) and *fair* (market or carnival).
- Homophony consists of words with the same pronunciation yet different meaning such as: *to, too,* and *two*; *there, their, they're,* and *by, bye, buy.*
- Heteronomy consists of words with the same spelling but are different in meaning and pronunciation such as *close* (as in near) and *close* (to shut), *read* (to read as in present tense) and *read* (to have read as in past tense), and *wind* (air movement) and *wind* (to coil).
- Polysemy consists of words that are spelled the same way, with two distinctive yet similar meanings, as is the case with *milking* (milking it for all its worth and the process of obtaining milk or milking the cow) and *wood* (a piece of a tree and an area of land with many trees).
- Capitonmy consists of words with the same spelling although are different in meaning (when one is capitalized, it can sometimes change in pronunciation) as in the case of the following: Job—a biblical figure and job—a form of employment; Lima—capital of Peru and lima—a kind of bean; August—the eighth month of the year and august—glorious, monumental, or stately.

Children in this phase of spelling development are using, manipulating, and in the process of figuring out homonyms. By this stage of spelling development, children are certainly able to spell these easy words. However, statistics show that *to*, *too*, and *two*; and *there*, *their*, and *they're* are among the most frequently misspelled words in Grades One through Six (Buchanan, 1989). In order to understand this concept and use the correct spelling, children must use word meaning to give the correct spelling. Children often misspell homophones because the words they write, albeit actual and conventional words, are wrong in meaning.

## MEANING-BASED WORD STUDY

Synonyms are a group of words with similar or identical connotation or meaning that are also interchangeable, for example: girl: babe, dame, female, lady, miss, schoolgirl; play: activity, drama, game, pastime; and run: amble, drive, sprint, and race.

Themes are groups of words that are compiled and organized in many different ways according to some form of content or meaning. These can include classifications such as: mathematical strands (numbers, patterns and relations, shape and space, and statistics and probability); genres (fantasy, historical fiction, humor, mystery, science fiction); continuums such as: gigantic, large, big, average, small, tiny, minute; and antonyms (opposites) such as: intriguing and dull, amusing and serious, swift and slow.

Units are groups of words that not only include synonyms and themes but any word unit that has words related to a central or focused word, for example: word origins, word neologisms, and plurals.

Word origins can make the English language more complicated to learn and understand since over the years, people have joined prefixes and then changed the spelling. For example, *assist, applaud, approach, attend,* and *attain* were all originally spelled with the prefix *ad*, such that assist was spelled *adsist*, applaud was spelled *adplaud*, approach was spelled *adproach*, and so on. Thus, researching word origins becomes an important element in the spelling process.

When investigating word origins and their history, spellers learn to understand the spelling changes and the "revised" spelling has meaning for them. More specifically, understanding word derivatives' history and origin helps children become attuned to the changes; then they can decide for themselves if a word such as *applaud* is spelled with one *p* or two.

Word neologisms relate to the formation of new words, which include the following: compound words, coining, clipping, portmanteau words, acronyms, eponyms, onomatopoeia words, oxymorons, and contractions.

Compound words are the formation of one word from two words, for example: software, snowman, and quicksand. There are three forms of compound words:

- The Closed Form—words that are blended together such as childlike, basketball, cowboy, notebook.
- The Hyphenated Form—words that are joined together by a hyphen such as mother-in-law, ten-year-old, T-shirt.
- The Open Form—words that are written together with word spacing though are considered as one word such as post office, middle class, step sister, high school.

The word is considered a compound word only when the two smaller words relate to the newly created word. Straightforward basic combinations such as *milkman* present no difficulty; descriptive compounds such as *blackberry* and *blackbird* are allowed in the form of specializations; while words such as *butterflies* and *chestnuts* are debatable because the two smaller words give no clues to their identity.

Coining is the creation of new words on purpose. John Milton's *pandemonium* from *Paradise Lost* is a well-known and used coined word. Company trademark names such as Xerox, Levi's, and Kleenex are also coined words. The coined word *e-mail* comes from the words *electronic mail.* Clipping is the deliberate shortening of words such as: *pants—pantaloons, gym—gymnasium, bike—bicycle, memo—memorandum, stereo—stereophonic,* and *photo—photograph.*

Portmanteau words are when a new word is created by combining two words to make a smaller word. For example, *smog* is derived from the words *fog* and *smoke,* while *brunch* is derived from the words *breakfast* and *lunch.*

Acronyms are created by combining the initial letters or syllables of several words. The word *scuba* is created from the words *self-contained underwater breathing apparatus.* IKEA, the name of the European superstore, was named after its founder; the acronym IKEA is made up of the initials of his name (Ingvar Kamprad or IK); in addition to the initials of Elmtaryd, the family farm where he was born, and Agunnaryd, a nearby village in the province of Småland.

Eponyms are words derived from a person's name such as the word *maverick*. This word derives from Samuel A. Maverick, a Texas lawyer who refused to brand his cattle. Washington, D.C. is named after George Washington, the United States' first president. The word *gargantuan* derives from Gargantua, a French Renaissance writer's (François Rabelais) fictional character. The term *paralympian* is a new word derived from the words *Olympian* and *paraplegic* and is used to refer to a competitor in the Special Games.

Onomatopoeia words are words created from a figure of speech that echoes the sound it is describing, for example: meow, bowwow, plop, bang, and click.

Oxymorons are words made up of a combination of contradictory and opposing terms such as: cruel kindness. The term "oxymoron" itself is an oxymoron. It is a Greek term derived from oxy ("sharp") and moros ("dull"). Its meaning is: that which is sharp and dull.

Contractions are shortened words made from two words by replacing one or more letters with an apostrophe. The meaning does not change. Examples are: don't, you're, and it's. To use and understand contractions, children must relate their spelling to meaning in order to produce the correct spelling; for example, the word *shouldn't* means should not.

Plurals are a grammatical classification meaning or comprising of more than one. Plurals include the following:

- Regular plurals: The most common regular plural form of most nouns is created simply by adding the letter *s* to the end of the word. For example: *chair—chairs, book—books,* and *boy—boys.*
- Words that end in *ch, x, s,* or *s*-like sounds, however, form their plurals by adding *es* to the end of the word. Examples include: dish—dishes, peach—peaches, box—boxes, and kiss—kisses.
- Nouns ending in *o* present a peculiar problem. In many cases, nouns ending in *o* require an *es* to make them plural, as in nouns ending in *o* preceded by a consonant, for example: tomatoes, heroes, and mosquitoes. In many other instances, the noun ending in *o* is pluralized by just adding *s*, as in clipped or shortened words, (for example, memos,

photos, video, piano, and zoo) and nouns ending in *o* that are preceded by a vowel (for example: cameos, duos).

- In nouns ending with a *y* preceded by a consonant, you change the *y* to an *i* and add *es*, for example: baby—babies, candy—candies, and cherry—cherries. This does not apply to proper nouns. Proper nouns form their plurals by the addition of *s*.
- Irregular plurals are any other plural forms. There are many.
- Mutated irregular noun plurals are plurals originating from Old English, for example: child—children, foot—feet, mouse—mice, and goose—geese.
- Irregular noun plurals are plurals that maintain their Latin or Greek form, for example: nucleus—nuclei, fungus—fungi, vertex—vertices, and phenomenon—phenomena.
- There are other irregular noun plurals from other foreign origins such as: the French words *beau—beaux*; the Hebrew words *cherub—cherubim/cherubs*; and the Inuktitut words *igloo—igloos, anorak—anoraks*, and *Inuk—Inuit*. The Japanese, Chinese, and Korean languages have collective nouns but not grammatical word plural forms, for example: kimonos, samurai, and sensei.
- To change words that end in *f* or *fe* to the plural form, one usually changes the *f* to *v* and adds *s* or *es*. Examples include: knife—knives, leaf—leaves, self—selves, and life—lives.
- Plural nouns used to qualify other noun elements are generally written in singular form, even though they mean more than one, for example: dog catcher, department store, sixteen-foot ceiling, and fifty-dollar bill.
- Plural usage to qualify nouns is more common with irregular plurals. For example, women killers are women who kill and woman killers are people who kill women.
- In general, closed formed compound words (words that are blended together) form plurals by the addition of *s* at the end of the word. For example: schoolhouses, fingernails, and notebooks. The same applies to compound words that end in *ful*. For example: truckfuls, handfuls, and armfuls.
- Hyphenated compound plurals or open form compounds are combination words where the plural *s* is attached to the element that is being pluralized, usually the primary noun (header), for example: brothers-in-law, half sisters, full moons, and commanders-in-chief.

- In compound words where both elements are considered primary nouns and the first header has an irregular plural form, both elements are pluralized, for example: menservants and women doctors.
- However, a compound word where both headers are considered primary and the first header is standard and not irregular, the final header is pluralized. Examples include: city-states and nurse practitioners.
- In other plural compound words with three or more words that are considered as headers, one of which is in irregular plural form, only the irregular plural is changed, for example: men-at-war, children of the street.
- Plurals of peoples' nationalities have different spellings. Generally, one can add *s* and *ish* to the root word of people's names, for example: Dane becomes Danes or Danish; Finn becomes Finns or Finnish; and Spaniard becomes Spaniards or Spanish.
- Other peoples' names that end in *ese* are not pluralized. As in the words: Chinese and Japanese. Other peoples' names that have no plural form include Swiss, Québécois, and many Native American names.
- Then, there are collective nouns that are words denoting a group or collection of nouns. Examples of these are: a cache of jewels, an army of ants, a drove of cattle, a rockery of penguins, and a school of fish.
- There are lexical collectives. They are classified according to count and mass nouns. Mass nouns are groups by definition that show no plurals, such as: footwear, deer, garbage, fish (and many individual fish names: cod, mackerel, and trout), luggage, and traffic.
- Count nouns have singular and plural form, such as: suitcase—suitcases, laugh—laughs, and animal—animals. Some nouns have two plurals, one referring to several things considered individually and the other referring to several things considered collectively, for example: cloths—clothes, person—people, dice—dies, and fish—fishes.
- Numerical expressions are usually written in singular and can be considered as plural if the individuals within a numerical group are acting individually, for example: "Seventy percent of the student population is graduating this summer" or "Seventy percent of the student population have passed their provincial exams." Notice the change in verb form from singular to plural.
- Sometimes objects appear to be plural although the verb is singular. In the example, "My daughter is very good at gymnastics," the noun gymnastics ends in an *s* and sounds plural, but the verb *is*, is singular.

- Then there are possessives, plural nouns indicating "possession" or belonging to. Apostrophes are used to form plurals when showing possession. When we refer to specific letters as in, "Sara got all *A*'s on her year-end report card," an apostrophe is used to show possessive plurals. When creating a plural form of a word that refers to the word itself, such as, "Remember not use too many *and*'s or *then*'s in your writing" or "That is the dog's water dish," an apostrophe is used again to show a possessive plural.

- When the nouns are plurals to begin with and you want to show possession, in most cases, you simply add the apostrophe after the *s* or *es*, as in: "This is the Newburns' house" or "The students' desks were all in the horseshoe formation." To show possession in plural nouns that are irregular, you add the apostrophe before you add the *s* as in: "These are the children's report cards" and "Kate has started a women's line of perfume."

I didn't know plurals were so complex. How about you? Due to these many peculiarities, variations, and exceptions, most dictionaries provide several acceptable spellings for plurals.


## READING IDEAS AND ACTIVITIES

This is the time to help enhance and expand your child's reading. Choose literature-rich books and articles on word study. Take your child with you to the library and research books and articles about word meaning and origin. You can also search the Internet for the same.

At the same time, it is a good idea to take the personal books your child is reading and together create different word study activities and games from excerpts within them.

*Econo-saver*: Remember to use the library to borrow books and always check out book and garage sales for great used books.

As mentioned previously, one is never too old a reader or too independent a person to have a story read aloud. There are so many advantages to this activity: a sense of belonging, a bond, oratorical speech development, listening skill development, comprehension, and pure untouched enjoyment to name a few. Always encourage and provide reading aloud activities and opportunities.

# Writing Ideas and Activities

## WRITTEN WORK

Have children research the dictionary, encyclopedia, thesaurus, and other reference material at the library, or surf the Internet while examining and applying word study. With the gathered material, you can plan interesting, meaningful, and educational ways of presenting the information. Children at this level of learning enjoy and remember material that they have put together in a meaningful manner and to which they can relate. Some ideas could include:

### Report Writing

With the gathered information, create written reports presented in various book forms. For example, you can create a report on a blank cube. Each side would present a subtopic of your chosen word study. The cube can be made out of paper, card stock, or even wood. Search the Internet for report writing cube masters.

Don't just get stuck in the box. Think outside the box. Have your child choose a 3-D shape or object that symbolizes some meaning related to her word study. Have her create her report on it. My daughter did a book report on "The Face on the Milk Carton." She designed a large milk carton and made a report college with it.

Design an accordion-style folding book by folding a legal-sized sheet of paper in half lengthwise, then in half widthwise, and finally open it, still folded lengthwise. Fold the paper again widthwise by bringing both ends to the folded middle and bending, after which you bend it again from the middle. And there you go; your accordion-style book is made. Be creative and imaginative. Search the library and Internet for book-making ideas.

### Interactive Media Project

Another idea is to make a tri-fold, newspaper, video, or PowerPoint presentation of your chosen word study. Be resourceful and use a combination of several media. Try writing a script and presenting it live or on video. My daughter made a science video about germs; she wrote a script and made a video. She had a blast and her abstract study on germs was made more concrete and memorable by the very nature of the project.

*Econo-saver:* Tri-folds can be purchased at office supply stores. You can make your own by simply reusing a large cardboard box, opening it up, removing one side, and cutting to the length you need. Then using paint or material, paint or cover the entire tri-fold—ads and all.

## Family Night Reporter

Have your child prepare, report, and discuss the particulars of his word study for the week. You can have him teach and "educate" the family. When appropriate, make sure that he tries and focuses the direction of his presentation using the 5 *W*'s + H questions as a framework (i.e., who, what, where, when, why, and how?).

## Editors

This is a great time for your child to focus on editing his or her own personal writing. Have your child become the editor of his or her own work. Encourage and practice proofreading. Keep in mind that there are several drafts involved in the writing process from first draft to a final good copy. The first draft is strictly for writing ideas down on paper. Subsequent drafts are for editing purposes until a final, good copy is reached. Don't be concerned with correct spelling in initial writing drafts. Children often become too concerned with the mechanics of their writing and their creative ideas; willingness to write and take risks become suppressed.

Good copies and published works should contain perfect spelling. When children are writing their drafts, make sure to teach them to read, check, and ask several different people to conference with them. You can have them look for spelling errors, awkward sentence structure, grammatical mistakes, incomplete thoughts, confusing thoughts, and so on, all of which are activities that focus on word study. COPS is a great acronym I use with my students when editing.

C: Capitalization
O: Overused words
P: Punctuation
S: Spelling

For spelling checks I always have my students read their words in their writing back to front. This isolates every word in their writing and does not permit the mind to skip ahead.

Teach students to use resources such as unabridged dictionaries, thesauruses, and grammar and reference material. These are important for spelling attempts and spelling inquiries, as well as word knowledge and understanding. Every household should have at least one of each. Furthermore, you should keep a personal dictionary at hand. Please refer to chapter 2 for the student word book and words–dictionary-making ideas. This consists of a lined notebook for entering, alphabetically, those words that a child has spelled constantly incorrectly, word families that he or she has had difficulty with, suggestions from spelling conferences, examples of groups of words that illustrate a certain spelling convention, and so forth.

The ultimate purpose of writing is to record thoughts and ideas. Spelling is the vehicle for getting a message across. We need to keep in mind—that our concern about spelling changes as our intended audience changes. We have scribbled notes and ideas, drafts, good copies, and even published writing. When you write a grocery list, chances are that you give little, if any, thought toward spelling. If you were to write a letter to the Prime Minister of Canada, you can be sure that you'd want the spelling to be perfect.

## FUN AND GAMES

Children at this age are enthusiastic about and intrigued with creating and performing games and activities, as well as researching and finding tidbit information—and are more than competent to do so. It is a great idea to help your child gather and collect the materials needed to make a game. Build the game and test it together, making any necessary modifications to play the game with family and friends. The following are examples of word study games to get you started. The variety and number of games you can come up with depend on your imagination. Go for it. Indulge.

### Word Race to a Hundred

Make a deck of words, which could be root words, contractions, homonyms, neologisms, affixes, plurals, and so on. The first player draws a card from the deck and calls it out. Each player then has a minute to write as many related words as they can think of. Each player gets five points for every legitimate word he or she has created and has a turn to draw a word from the deck. The first player to reach a hundred wins the game.

### Word Study Charades

Decide on the theme for your word study, for example: homophonies, synonyms, word neologisms, and affixes. Then further refine the word study to a specific category, such as synonyms that start with the letter *g*. Write several words, phrases, and so forth on blank cards, which all must relate to the chosen theme. Have a person draw a word card and act out or draw clues about the word for others to guess. A point is given to the person who both guesses and spells the word correctly.

### Compound Word Dominoes

Start with a compound word. Take the last small word in the compound word and create a new compound word. Keep building. See how long of a domino train you can make. Examples include: aircrafts, craftsman, manpower, powerhouse, housework, workshop, and shopkeeper.

### Compound Submarine Sandwiches

Create a deck consisting of compound words and make a rummy game with the words you are studying. Have your child choose a card from the deck, for example, "snowman." Have him build a sandwich from the two words that make up the compound word. Other examples are: snowball, snowshoes, snowmobile, snowfall, policeman, gentleman, businessman, chairman, spokesman, layman, and freshman. See how many new words you can make for your Submarine Sandwich.

### Word Study Flip Book

Start by choosing what area of word study is to be your focus. If you choose to study affixes, for example, you need to make category cards of prefixes, suffixes, and root word pages (for the flip book). Keep in mind that whatever word study you choose to focus on, choose only three categories. This keeps the game simple and noncomplicated.

To begin making your flip book pages, take an 8½" × 11" blank sheet of paper. Fold it evenly into three equal sections. Outline each section with marker, making each section the same size and as large as possible. This is your master.

Now photocopy the master many times onto card stock paper. Fold pages into three equal sections, cut each section on its fold, and hole punch inside the top of each rectangle.

You are ready to write on your card stock flip book pages. Write on the pages according to the game's needs. Organize the pages into the categories and place in a three-ring binder. This allows for easy "flipping" of the pages in their individual categories.

You now have your Flip Book, and you may begin to challenge each other. To do so, you make new words from the root words with suffixes or prefixes by "flipping" each of the individual category pages. Check with the dictionary to verify the words.

### I'm Going on a Camping Trip

To play this game, start by saying, "I am going on a camping trip. Do you want to come?" The next player must say, "Yes, I do. What can I bring?"

The person who starts the game must say an item they want bring on the camping trip, and this word must have the correct combination of his secret sequence (which the rest of the players must figure out). For example, let's say, the secret combination is as follows: each item must begin with the next letter of the alphabet. You start the game by saying: "You may bring an apple."

The next person must repeat the item and add a new one to the list. For example, the next player might then say, "I am going on a camping trip, and I am bringing an apple and peach. May I come?"

Your response is, "No, you may not come." If the person mentions an item that begins with the letter B, such as banana, he stays in the game, and then you have to respond with, "Yes, you may."

Following this, you give that person an opportunity to guess the secret sequence. If that person's guess is wrong, the play continues to the next person, and you repeat the entire sequence, in order to date. For example, you would say, "I am going on a camping trip, and I am going to bring an apple. Do you want to come?"

It is now the next player's turn, and he says, "Yes, I do. What may I bring?"

The person who started the game (you in this example) then says the entire sequence once again and adds an item to the list. For example, you would say, "You may bring an apple and a book."

Then that other player would respond, "I am going on a camping trip, and I am going to bring an apple, a book, and a camera. May I come?" Your response would have to be, "Yes, you may come."

The complete round continues until someone has guessed the correct secret sequence and is declared the winner. The winner becomes the starter of the next game.

Other examples of secret sequences might be: words that begin with the same sound, words that are opposites, position words (i.e., up, down, on, off, under, over) and others; use whatever would be appropriate in accordance to the child's needs and what you have been studying. Keep in mind the level of knowledge of the child. This game can be easily modified according to ability and needs levels.

### Word Study Toss

Make two separate grids out of paper liners to line two shoe boxes. Each paper liner should have nine equal-sized grid boxes. On each paper liner, write your word formations. For example, if you chose to study suffixes, put nine suffixes (one per grid) on one liner and nine root words (one per grid) on the other.

Place the paper liners inside each shoe box. Gather two game markers (i.e., pennies, beans, or beads), pencil and paper. Create new words by throwing the game markers in the boxes, one in each box, and combining the suffix with the root word.

To verify and determine a correct word, check with the dictionary. If the word is correct, points are given. You can predetermine the point value for each new word and the game point number before the game.

You can change the grid liners to create new word formations, just as is done in Bingo. Other word-formations can be studied and created, but remember to keep in mind that your word study choice must have only two variants (one for each box).

### Paper Word Wash Line

Begin by choosing what area of word study is to be your focus. If you choose to study compound words, for example, you need to make two sets of category word cards that, when joined together, make a compound word. Keep in mind that whatever word study you choose to focus on, you should create as many sets of category cards as there are variants. Each category card set must be written on different colored construction paper.

Gather some clothespins and two laundry baskets (plastic containers) and create a clothesline from yarn or string. Start hanging out the clothes (words that, when combined, make new compound words).

Draw a word from each of the two containers without looking. Place them together on the clothesline and then check to see if the new compound word is actually a compound word. Players get points for every legitimate compound word they make.

### Word Study Treasure Hunt

Set up a house hunt or newspaper hunt, creating clues and searching for related objects or words reviewing the concepts. Have your child look for a particular word study, such as finding examples of things that end in *ng*. Set a specific time limit. Have a race against the clock to see who can come up with the most words or objects using a particular learned concept.

**Figure 5.3.    Nicole, Natalie, and Gillian**

### Who Am I Riddles

Together with your child, choose a word study focus and make some riddles. When writing riddles, remember to start from the back and work toward the beginning. Think of the answer first; next, imagine the answer talking to you, hence the, "I am beginning . . ." Be specific, talk about the object/word, itself: what it looks like, sounds like, what it likes to do, any interesting or unique qualities, and so forth.

Then turn these clues into a poem. You can choose to make it rhyme, if you want. Make sure that the clues are appropriate for your audience with regards to subject matter and acuity.

Riddles are played between two or more people—and they are a combination of wit and poetry. When the game is being played with two people only, players take turns presenting their riddles and answering their opponents' riddles. An incorrect answer gives the riddle writer a point; a correct answer gives the responder a point. The game goes back and forth until a predetermined final score is reached. Take note that vague or nonsensible riddles are not allowed.

If you're playing a multi-player game, you can add a judge. That person is allowed to accept or reject the riddle on grounds of vagueness or sensibility. Furthermore, the judge may award "ahh-ha" points when the responder provides an answer that is not what the riddle maker chose, but is equally good or even sounds better.

### Word Study Comprehension Game

In preparation for this game, choose several comprehension questions regarding a certain word study focus. Write a comprehension question on card stock—one per card. Make a deck of cards, as well as a game board, playing pieces, and spinner. Search the Internet for game board and spinner masters. You'll also need some dice. When all material is gathered, you're ready to play. This game is best played with four or more people.

To start the game, shuffle the deck and place the cards face down on the table. Take the dice and roll. The person with the highest number goes first, and all plays run clockwise. Place all players on start.

The first player rolls the dice, then moves the number of spaces indicated on the dice and follows the instructions. If the player is told to draw a question from the deck, he must draw a card and then answer the question. If he answers correctly, the player remains on the space and rolls again. The play continues until he is told to lose a turn or answers a question incorrectly. If a player answers a question incorrectly, he must return to his previous space and forfeit his turn. The game continues until someone reaches the finish line.

*Econo-saver:* Collect and recycle old birthday, Christmas and greeting cards. Cut out the backs and use them for all your blank card needs.

*Econo-saver:* Organize all games into sturdy baggies and file them in file folders and boxes. Label everything clearly with permanent marker, for easy future access.

Word study should include a variety of word games and activities. These games and activities provide enjoyment and excitement to a child's learning. They engage the child in critical thinking as he or she examines the information, corresponding concepts, or word structure, and they allow for experimentation with the written word, providing children with challenging situations, rather than the ordinary drill and memory work.

Children involved in these games and activities become explorers of words, thus utilizing their innate curiosity, and this becomes the springboard for word discovery and understanding. When participating in word study, you should help them collect and interpret the needed information. Discuss word formation, patterns, vocabulary, grammar, word usage, and word meaning, and above all else, have fun.

In any single spelling attempt, a person must be able to think of the word he wishes to spell. He must be able to see in his mind what the word looks like. The person must have available to him and be able to choose certain strategies to help him select a proper spelling. That is, he must be able to use word meaning and context and to match sound-to-letter sequences. He must have an understanding of word patterns and function.

Furthermore, he must be able to reproduce standard graphic symbols we call letters to transcribe his visual thoughts onto a writing surface. He must do all of this while remembering in his mind the word he wishes to spell.

Lastly, he must judge and decide for himself if the word is correct or if he needs to go through the process again.

Involved in any spelling attempt is always the reading and writing process.

# Appendix

## Table A.1. Stages of spelling development

| Gillet and Temple[a] | Read 1986[b] | Gentry[c] | Buchanan[d] | Beers and Beers 1977[e] | Henderson and Templeton 1986[f] |
|---|---|---|---|---|---|
| Prephonemic Spelling Stage | Prephonetic Stage | Pre-communicative Stage | Prephonetic Stage | Prephonetic Stage | Stage I |
| *—Knowledge of form and function of print*   *—Random strings of letters, pictures, numbers* | | | | | |
| Early Phonetic Spelling Stage | Phonetic Stage | Semiphonetic Stage | Early Phonetic Stage | Early Phonetic Stage | Stage II |
| *—Some matching of sounds and letters*   *—Words limited to 1–3 letters*   *—Knowledge of left to right* | | | | | |
| Letter – Name Spelling Stage | Grapho – phonetic Stage | Phonic Stage | Advanced Phonetic Stage | Phonetic Stage | |
| *—Word boundaries established*   *—Letters assigned closely approximate sounds* | | | | | |
| Transitional Spelling Stage | Transitional, Phonetic, Orthographic Stage | Transitional Spelling Stage | Phonetic Stage | Structural Stage | Stage III |
| *—Conventional Spelling more consistent*   *—Knowledge of letter patterns*   *—Vowel knowledge* | | | | | |
| Correct Spelling Stage | Semantic/Syntactic Morphemic/Syntactic Stage | Correct Spelling Stage | Correct Spelling Stage | Meaning/Derivational Spelling Stage | Stage IV/V |
| *—Can spell most words needed correctly*   *—Can recognize words*   *—Polysyllabic words*   *—Levels of automaticity* | | | | | |

[a]Gillet, J. W., and Temple, C. (1982). *Understanding reading problems: Assessment and instruction*. Toronto, ON: Little, Brown and Co.

[b]Read, Charles. (1986). *Children's Creative Spelling*. London: Routledge and Kegan Paul.

[c] Gentry, J. R. (1987). *Spel . . . Is a four-letter word*. Richmond Hill, Ontario: Scholastic-TAB Publications.

[d]Buchanan, E. (1989). *Spelling for whole language classrooms*. Winnipeg, MA: Whole Language Consultants.

[e]Beers, J. W. and C. S. Beers, (1977). The logic behind children's spelling. *The Elementary School Journal*, 77(3): 238–42.

[f]Henderson, E. H., and S. Templeton. (1986). A developmental perspective of formal spelling instruction through alphabet, pattern, and meaning. *Elementary School Journal*, 86(3): 304–16.

# Glossary

**Affixes**: the creation of new words by adding to the original root words. There are either derivational or inflectional.

*Derivational* is a word formation process whereby the new word is derived from another existing word by adding affixes and changing its part of speech; for example:

- Adjective to noun, as in: close—closeness
- Adjective to verb, as in: visual—visualize
- Noun to adjective, as in: joy—joyous
- Noun to verb, as in: beauty—beautify
- Verb to adjective, as in: defend—defendable
- Verb to noun, as in: occur—occurrence

Derivation may also occur without any change of form. For example, in the words medical and medicine, the *c* in both words sounds different—one is a hard *c* and the other is a soft *c*. When children understand that two words are derivative of each other, they can think back, make the connection, and are able to "come-up" with the correct spelling.

*Inflectional* is the modification or changing of a word to indicate grammatical information, such as gender as in the case of actor—actress; the verb tenses such as: hand—handed, think—thought, write—wrote—written, and sing—sang—sung—singing; noun plurals such as: ring—rings and boy—boys; irregular plurals such as: child—children, mouse—mice and foot—feet; adjectives such as: tall—taller and happy—happiest; or first person such as *I* or *me*, second person such as *you*, and third person such as *he, him, his, she, her, they, it*, and so on.

The common English affixes are:

- Prefixes—before the root word (they mostly come from Latin): attend, exit, redo, and unhappy
- Suffixes—after the root: government, condemnation, useless, friendship, telephone, and quickly
- Infixes—within the root word: sang, song, and sing. It is only the vowel that is changing. Other infixes are common in slang words/language such as hip-hop slang. Other examples include: *hizouse* or *hizzy* for *house*, *crizib* for *crib* and *driz* for *drink*; words created from the TV show "The Simpsons" such as *sophistimacated, saxomaphone*, and *edumacation*; language games such as "pig Latin" and some technical terminology.
- Circumfixes—before and after root word: evaporate, enlighten, and embolden
- Suprafixes—a kind of affix in which the pronunciation, meaning, or parts of speech (the noun and related verb) of a word changes by changing the accent or stressed syllable. Examples are: 'produce (noun) and pro'duce (verb), 'discount (noun) and dis'count (verb), and 'object (noun) and ob'ject (verb).
- Simulfixes—a type of affix that changes one or more existing phonemes (the smallest unit of sound) in order to modify and change the meaning of a morpheme (the smallest meaningful unit in the grammar of a language). Examples of simulfixes in English are generally considered irregularities from singular to plural form such as: mouse—mice, man—men, louse—lice, tooth—teeth, and woman—women, etc.

**Antonym**: words that are opposite in meaning: hot and cold, fast and slow

**Apostrophe**: a punctuation mark. It marks and defines letter omissions and noun and pronoun possessives. For instance: *Roberta's hat* or using *doesn't* for *does not*.

**Book types**: different methods of presenting and shaping a book. For example:

- Big Books—large over-sized books with enlarged print and illustrations. They are meant to be enjoyed by a group of people usually in a shared reading environment.

- Information Books (also called nonfiction)—true informative stories about real characters, places, and events
- Picture Books—have little or few words; the illustrations tell the story
- Taped Books—recorded stories on cassette tapes or CDs. They are usually recorded by storytellers and actors.
- Palm Books—small-sized, interactive books that fit in the palm of your hand
- Peek-A-Boo Books—interactive books that have pictures and messages hidden behind flaps
- Push and Pull Books—interactive books that have cardboard flaps which the reader pushes or pulls to see hidden pictures or messages
- Squeeze-me, and Touch and Feel Books—interactive books that have pages to squeeze or textures to touch
- Rebus stories—substituting pictures for hard-to-read words that students decode. For example: I ♥ you.

**Compound words:** words made up of two words joined together with no letters left out. The new compound word has a different meaning than the original two words.

**Consonant:** the letters other than *a, e, i, o, u,* and sometimes *y* of the Greek alphabet

**Consonant blends** (sometimes known as a cluster): when two or more consonants fuse or blend together, while maintaining their individual sounds. For example: blanket, plastic, treat, stripe, and grand.

**Consonant digraphs:** when two consonants combine to make one sound. The most common consonant digraphs are *ch, sh, th, ph,* and *wh.*

**Contractions:** shortened words made from two words by replacing one or more letters with an apostrophe. The meaning does not change.

**Genre:** Different types of literature; essentially, they are:

- Biography—stories about real people's lives and events
- Fantasy—stories that include characters and events that cannot happen in real life
- Fiction—stories that are made up and did not really happen
- Historical fiction—stories that could have happened in the past, but they didn't
- Mystery—stories that have a question or crime that must be solved
- Nonfiction—stories about real characters, places and events. They are usually written with the purpose of providing true information.

- Poetry—uses rhythm and often rhymes as a method of exploring feelings and senses to convey experiences, ideas, and emotions in a vivid and imaginative way
- Realistic fiction—stories that are written as if they could happen today
- Science fiction—stories that take place in the future, and make you think about what could happen by reason of scientific developments
- Folklore, myths, and legends—traditional stories that have been passed down by storytellers from one generation to the next. Now they are being written down in tangible form.
- Humor—stories written with the purpose of being funny, with hilarious characters, events, and settings
- Classic—stories enjoyed by many people over many years. They are often studied by experts in literature.

**Grapheme:** a written symbol or sequences of written symbols used to represent a single phoneme or unit of sound with meaning

**Homonym:** a group of words that have the same spelling, pronunciation, or both but have a different meaning. For example: to, too, and two; bark (a noise a dog makes or a part of a tree); and bear and bare.

**Inquiry-based learning:** an educational philosophy whereby children are engaged in their own learning through an inquiry process. Their learning and understanding is led by student generated questions and queries.

**Inventive spelling:** nonstandard spelling. It is the practice of permitting students to write how they think a particular word is spelled, rather than the way it actually is spelled.

**Letter:** a symbol or character that is conventionally used in writing and printing to represent a speech sound and that is part of an alphabet

**Morpheme:** the smallest linguistic unit that has meaning

**Orthography:** a set of symbols written by following a system of standards (i.e., spelling, grammar, capitalization, and punctuation)

**Parts of speech:** a traditional classification of words according to their functions to maintain meaning in writing. It includes nouns, pronouns, verbs, adjectives, adverbs, prepositions, conjunctions, interjections, and sometimes articles.

- Noun—the name of a person, place, thing, idea, living creature, quality, or action. Examples include: girl, boy, bed, dream, tree, cat, neighborhood, and help.

- Verb—a word which describes an action (doing something) or a state (being something): walk, run, write, think, love, and wish
- Adjective—a word that describes a noun. It adds detail to your writing. In general, adjectives go before the noun. They also may appear after a noun or a linking verb; for instance: beautiful, amazing, huge, gentle, hasty, Canadian, long, faithful, strong, squishy, rainy, silent, hilarious, grungy.
- Adverb—a word that describes a verb. It tells you how something is done. It may also tell you when or where something happened. It usually ends in *ly*, as found in: gingerly, swiftly, intelligently, gone, and wherever.
- Pronoun—used to replace or substitute nouns. They have a very general reference as in *she, who, this*, and *I*. Pronouns keep nouns from being overworked or redundant.
- Personal pronouns—stand-ins for specific persons or things. They change form to indicate a person (first, second, or third person), number, gender, and case (whether it is subjective, objective, or possessive). Personal pronouns are the pronouns we use the most: I, me, us, ours, yourself, he, her, itself, them, and their.
- Interrogative pronouns—ask questions. They interrogate and challenge the bystander. In English, there are five interrogative pronouns: what, which, who, whom, and whose.
- Demonstrative pronouns (this, that, these and those)—substitute-nouns that when placed maintain meaning by reason of its context. They also indicate whether the noun is plural or singular.
- Indefinite pronouns—refer to people, places, or things in a general or unspecific way: singular indefinite pronouns (another, anybody, everything, nothing, one, other, something, etc.), plural indefinite pronouns (both, few, many, others, and several), and singular or plural indefinite pronouns (all, any, more, most, and none).
- Conjunction—used to join two words, phrases, or sentences together. Examples include: but, so, because, or, however.
   Preposition—usually comes before a noun, pronoun, or noun phrase.
- It joins the noun to a part of the sentence and modifies the verb, nouns, and adjectives: on, in, by, with, to, since, under, through, at.
- Interjection—often stands in isolation. Interjections are words which express emotion or surprise, and are usually followed by exclamation marks: Ouch!, Hello!, Hurray!, Ugh!, Oh no!, Good Grief! and Ha!
- Article—identifies a noun: the, a, an

**Pattern**: a group of letters, blends, digraphs, or affixes that, when combined, present meaning to a word spelling

**Phonemic awareness**: the ability to notice, think about, and work with the individual sounds in spoken words

**Phonemic segmentation**: the practice of hearing and counting the individual sounds heard in words

**Phoneme**: the smallest linguistic unit of sound with meaning

**Phonogram**: also known as word families, these are predictable patterns (chunks) within words

**Phonics**: is a method of teaching children how to read and spell by matching letters or groups of letters to related sounds

**Plurals**: a grammatical classification meaning or comprising of more than one. Plurals include the following:

- Regular plurals: The most common regular plural form of most nouns is created simply by adding the letter *s* to the end of the word. For example: chair— chairs, book—books, and boy—boys.
- Words that end in *ch*, *x*, *s* or *s*-like sounds, however, form their plurals by adding *es* to the end of the word. Examples: dish—dishes, peach—peaches, box—boxes, and kiss—kisses.
- Nouns ending in *o* present a peculiar problem. In many cases, nouns ending in *o* require an *es* to make them plural, as in nouns ending in *o* preceded by a consonant; for example: tomatoes, heroes, and mosquitoes. In many other instances, the noun ending in *o* is pluralized by just adding *s*, as in clipped or shortened words; for example, memos, photos, video, piano, and zoo; also, nouns ending in *o* that are preceded by a vowel, for example: cameos, duos.
- For nouns ending with a *y* preceded by a consonant, change the *y* to *i* and add *es*. For example: baby—babies, candy—candies, and cherry—cherries. This does not apply to proper nouns. Proper nouns form their plurals by the addition of *s*.
- Irregular plurals: are any other plural forms, of which there are many
- Mutated irregular noun plurals are plurals originating from Old English, for example: child—children, foot—feet, mouse—mice, and goose—geese.
- Irregular noun plurals are plurals that maintain their Latin or Greek form, for example: nucleus—nuclei, fungus—fungi, vertex—vertices, and phenomenon—phenomena.

- There are other irregular noun plurals from other foreign origins, such as: the French words beau—beaux, the Hebrew words cherub—cherubim/cherubs, and the Inuktitut words igloo—igloos, anorak—anoraks, and Inuk—Inuit. The Japanese, Chinese, and Korean languages have collective nouns but not grammatical word plural forms, for example: kimonos, samurai, and sensei.

- To change words that end in *f* or *fe* to the plural form, one usually changes the *f* to *v* and adds *s* or *es*. Examples include: knife—knives, leaf—leaves, self—selves, and life—lives.

- Plural nouns used to qualify other noun elements are generally written in singular form, even though they mean more than one, for example: dog catcher, department store, sixteen-foot ceiling, and fifty-dollar bill. Plural usage to qualify nouns is more common with irregular plurals. For example, women killers are women who kill and woman killers are people who kill women.

- In general, closed formed compound words (words that are blended together) form plurals by the addition of *s* at the end of the word, for example: schoolhouses, fingernails, and notebooks. The same applies to compound words that end in *ful*, for example: truckfuls, handfuls, and armfuls.

- Hyphenated compound plurals or open-form compounds are combination words where the plural *s* is attached to the element that is being pluralized, usually the primary noun (header), for example: brothers-in-law, half sisters, full moons, and commanders-in-chief.

- In compound words in which both elements are considered primary nouns and the first header has an irregular plural form, both elements are pluralized, for example: menservants and women doctors.

- However, a compound word where both headers are considered primary and the first header is standard and not irregular, the final header is pluralized. Examples include: city-states and nurse practitioners.

- In other plural compound words with three or more words that are considered as headers, one of which is in irregular plural form, only the irregular plural is changed, for example: men-at-war, children of the street.

- Plurals of peoples' names have different spellings. Generally, one can add *s* and *ish* to the root word of people's names. For example: Dane becomes Danes or Danish; Finn becomes Finns or Finnish; and Spaniard becomes Spaniards or Spanish.

- Other peoples' names that end in *ese* are not pluralized. As in the words:
- Chinese and Japanese. Other peoples' names that have no plural form include Swiss, Québécois, and many Native American names.
- Then, there are collective nouns that are words denoting a group or collection of nouns. Examples of these are: a cache of jewels, an army of ants, a drove of cattle, a rockery of penguins, and a school of fish.
- There are lexical collectives. They are classified according to count and mass nouns. Mass nouns are groups by definition that show no plurals, such as: footwear, deer, garbage, fish (and many individual fish names: cod, mackerel, and trout), luggage, and traffic.
- Count nouns have singular and plural form, such as: suitcase—suitcases, laugh—laughs, and animal—animals. Some nouns have two plurals, one referring to several things considered individually and the other referring to several things considered collectively, for example: cloths—clothes, person—people, dice—dies, and fish—fishes.
- Numerical expressions are usually written in singular and can be considered as plural if the individuals within a numerical group are acting individually, for example: "Seventy percent of the student population is graduating this summer" or "Seventy percent of the student population have passed their provincial exams." Notice the shift in verb form from singular to plural.
- Sometimes nouns appear to be singular although the verb is plural. For example in, "My daughter is very good at gymnastics," the noun gymnastics ends in an *s* and sounds plural but the verb *is*, is singular.
- Then there are possessives, plural nouns indicating "possession" or belonging to. Apostrophes are used to form plurals when showing possession. When we refer to specific letters as in "Sara got all *A*'s on her year-end report card," an apostrophe is used to show possessive plurals. When creating a plural form of a word that refers to the word itself, such as, "Remember, do not use too many and's or then's in your writing" or "That is the dog's water dish," an apostrophe is used again to show the possessive plural.
- When the nouns are plurals to begin with, and you want to show possession, in most cases you simply add the apostrophe after the *s* or *es*, as in: "This is the Newburns' house" or "The students' desks were all in the horseshoe formation." To show possession in plural nouns that are irregular, you add the apostrophe before you add the *s* as in: "These are

the children's report cards" and "Kate has started a women's line of perfume."

**Poems**: a composition in verse rather than in prose. It is a method of exploring feelings and senses to convey experiences, ideas, and emotions in a vivid and imaginative way. Some examples are:

- Acrostic poem—a very easy and simple poem. It can be about any subject. The writing format is to put the letters that spell your subject down the left-hand side of your page. Using each letter as a starter; think of a word, phrase, or sentence that starts with that letter and describe your subject.
- Ballad—a narrative poem that tells a story. They are often used in songs and have a musical rhythm.
- The basic ballad form generally has four-line verses. The second and fourth lines rhyme, following an *abcb* rhythm pattern: *a* stands for one line ending, *b* for another, and *c* for another still. Seeing that there are two *b*'s in this pattern, means these are the two lines that rhyme.
- The meter (beats or rhythm) in a basic ballad follows a pattern of four-stressed syllables, three-stressed syllables, four-stressed syllables, and three-stressed syllables per stanza. Keep in mind that this is standard, not a must. Ballad writing is not an exact science. The important thing is that your ballad should have a smooth, song-like quality when you speak it aloud.
- Cinquain—a five-line poem. The first line is made up of one word, a subject, or noun. The second line is made up of two adjectives describing the subject or noun of line one. The third line is made up of adjectives describing the noun or subject of line one. The fourth line is made up of four words or a complete sentence describing the feelings of the subject or noun of line one. The fifth line is the same word repeated from the first line or a synonym of that word.
- Five *W*'s poem—another quick and simple nonrhyming poem. Each line of the poem answers one of the 5 *W*'s: Who? What? When? Where? Why?—as follows: Line 1: Who is the poem about? Line 2: What action is happening? Line 3: When does the action take place? A time: season, past, and future. Line 4: Where does the action take place? Setting. Line 5: Why does this action happen? A reason.

- Haiku poem—an unrhymed poem which originated from Japan. It captures the essence of a moment keenly perceived, and is usually about nature, involving words which paint a mental image. The rhythm focuses on syllabic patterning. It most often includes a three-line, 5-7-5 syllable pattern.
- Sensory poem—a poem using the five senses (sight, sound, touch, smell, and taste) as themes. Objects and their related emotions are brainstormed. It follows a six-line format. The first line names the object and where you were at the time of its sighting. Each subsequent line describes the emotions about the object, using: sounds like, smells like, tastes like, looks like, and feels like.
- Tongue twister: a specific type of poem. It is a phrase, sentence, or rhyme that presents challenges when orally spoken because it contains similar sounds. To create one, choose a name (using full names) or a nickname (names that begin with *b*, *d*, *l*, *m*, *p*, *s*, or *t* are easiest) and write it down on a piece of paper. Then, answer the following questions using words that begin with the same first sounds as the person's name: "What did she do?" "where," "when," "why," and "because".

**Possessives**: *'s* is used to indicate possession or belonging to a noun or pronoun.

**Reading strategies**: skills used to help emergent readers make connections between new knowledge and what they already know. Some examples are:

- DEAR—"Drop Everything and Read" is a time and reading intervention strategy whereby the reader must drop whatever they are doing and read whatever they have in front of them at that particular time.
- Guided reading—focuses on a small group of readers. The teacher and the readers each have his or her own text from the same book. The material is read in a group setting, with each individual participating in oral reading. Each reader's personal reading challenges are considered and addressed. The reading level is at the reader's instructional level, with the teacher guiding them with predicting context clues, letter and sound relationships, and word structure.
- Read aloud—a reading strategy where an experienced reader reads to someone or a group of people. Contrary to popular belief, reading aloud

should be performed with people of all ages and reading abilities. We are never too old to be read to.

• Shared reading—Shared reading is exactly what it sounds like—an interactive time when a story is read, shared, and collaboratively enjoyed by more than one person. It is a time for sharing, reading, laughing, and crying together! This can be carried out by simply encouraging echo reading (students repeating the words after the reader), choral reading (everyone reading at the same time together), or fill in-in-the-blank reading (the reader reading most of the text, only pausing when students are expected to fill in the blank—done mostly with rhyming words or other predictable words in the story).

• USSR—Uninterrupted and Sustained Silent Reading is a time and reading intervention strategy whereby a single person or group of readers read his or her own personal book for a specific amount of time. This time is to be a quiet time during which everyone is reading silently (reading in their head). USSR is also known as SQUIRT (Sustained Quiet Uninterrupted Reading Time) or FUR (Free and Uninterrupted Reading) or SSR (Sustained Silent Reading).

**Root word**: a unit of meaning within a word

**Spelling development**: the ability to search for and use common standard patterns and structure to obtain meaning in written language. It is generally categorized by five levels or stages (Gillet and Gentry, 1982): Prephonemic stage, Early Phonemic stage, Phonetic stage, Transitional stage and Standard stage.

**Student word book**: a student dictionary. Within its pages are pre-written high frequency words and blank lines for words that may be added in the future. The student comes to you for assistance with or to give you the spelling of a word and it is recorded in the book.

**Syllable**: the division of a word into units of spoken language that are comprised of more than a speech sound and each of which is made up of one or more vowel sounds.

**Syllable spelling patterns**: consist of the following six patterns:

• Closed syllables—which end in a consonant, and the vowel is generally short. They follow a vowel-consonant (vc): at, it, on, consonant-vowel-consonant (cvc): cat, hot, met, or consonant-vowel-consonant-consonant (cvcc) pattern: rabbit and napkin.

- Open syllables—end in a vowel sound and are generally long. They follow a vowel (v): *i* or *a*; consonant, vowel (cv): he, go, *va ca tion, mu sic*; and consonant-consonant-vowel (ccv) patterns: she, bright, *pro ba tion*.
- R-controlled syllables—when a vowel is followed by an *r* in the same syllable, that vowel is *r*-controlled. It is neither long nor short. *R*-controlled syllables *er, ir,* and *ur* often sound the same: *er*. For example: term, sir, fir, fur, far, for, sugar, and order. It is identified when a vowel is followed by the letter *r*; the letter affects the sound of the vowel. The vowel and the *r* appear in the same syllable: bird, turtle, and monster.
- Vowel team—*ai, ay, ea, ee, oa, oo, oi, oy, ou, ie,* and *ei*. Double vowels appear in the same syllable: boat and explain. Be careful of and study all *ea* double vowel combinations. These can represent three different sounds: the long *e* sound in *seat*, the short *e* sound in *death*, and the long *a* sounds in the word *great*.
- Vowel-silent *e* syllable—generally represents long-vowel sounds and has a vowel-consonant-silent *e* pattern, for example: compete, decide, and smile. The silent *e* at the end of the word makes the vowel preceding the consonant long.
- Consonant-*le* syllable—appears at the end of a word. The consonant-*le* forms the final syllable. The vowel *e* is silent. The consonant and the *le* combination cannot be segmented into two separate syllables. This is crucial to note when spelling. One must listen to the vowel which comes immediately before the consonant-*le* combination; if the vowel sound is short and there is another consonant before the consonant-*le* combination, in the word "single," there is no problem. The word is divided before the consonant-*le* and what is left; *sin*" is a closed syllable with a short vowel.
- However, if this vowel is short, and there is no consonant before the consonant-*le* combination, in "paddle," then the consonant in the consonant-*le* combination must be doubled. The *d* in paddle has to be doubled to close the syllable, thus keeping the vowel sound short. If the *d* were not doubled, the word would still have to have two syllables, *pa dle*, but the first syllable would be an open syllable in which the *a* would be long.

**Synonym**: A group of words with the same or similar meaning, for instance: family (ancestors, brethren, brood, children, clan, descendants, dynasty, forebears, generations, kin, race, relatives, and tribe) or happy (blissful, cheerful, delighted, ecstatic, gay, joyful, merry, and perky).

**Two-word rhyme** (echo-word reduplication): a rhyme created when two words, which are similar or nearly alike in sound, are put together, as in: hodgepodge, nitwit, ding dong, wishy-washy, and tick-tock. This can be done for example by changing the vowel, in *pitter-patter* or by changing the initial consonant or consonant cluster, in *willy-nilly*.

**Vowel**: the letters: *a, e, i, o, u,* and sometimes *y*. In the English language, there are three main types of vowels:

- Short vowels—the five single letters *a, e, i, o,* and *u,* when pronounced, sound like */a/* in *cat,* */e/* in *bet,* */i/* in *sit,* */o/* in *hot,* and */u/* in *cup.*
- Long vowels—say the names of the single letter vowels: *a, e, i, o, u,* (long *a* as in *baby*)
- Schwa vowels: neutral vowels that are neither long nor short and are found in unstressed or non-accented syllables. Generally, in words with more than two syllables, the schwa vowel is located in the middle syllable although not always, as in the case of the word *decimal*: the *i* and the *a* are both schwa vowels occurring in the middle and last syllable. For the most part, the schwa vowel sound in a two-syllable word is identified by the "*uh*" pronunciation and sound.

**Word**: a unit of language, consisting of one or more spoken sounds or their written representation that has meaning

**Word boundary**: the position before, after, and including the strings of letters within a word

**Word wall of fame**: a systematically organized collection of words that are displayed in large clear-print letters on a wall or other large display area.

# References

Beers, J. W. and C. S. Beers. (1977). *The logic behind children's spelling. The Elementary School Journal,* 77(3): 238–42.

Bourcier, G., and Clark, C. (1981). *An introduction to the history of the English language.* Cheltenham, England: Stanley Thornes.

Buchanan, E. (1989). *Spelling for whole language classrooms.* Winnipeg, MA: Whole Language Consultants.

Gentry, J. R. (1981). Learning to spell developmentally. *The Reading Teacher,* 34(4), 378–81.

———. (1982). An analysis of developmental spelling in GYNS at WRK. *The Reading Teacher,* 36(1), 192–200.

———. (1985). You can analyze developmental spelling—and here's how to do it! *Early Years K–8,* 15(9), 44–45.

———. (1987). *Spel . . . is a four letter word.* Richmond Hill, ON: Scholastic-TAB Publications.

———. (2000). A retrospective on inventive spelling and a look forward. *The Reading Teacher,* 54(3), 318–32.

———. (2007). *Breakthrough in reading and writing.* New York: Scholastic.

Gentry, J.R., and Gillet, J.W. (1993). *Teaching kids to spell.* Portsmouth, NH: Heinemann Publishers.

Gillet, J. W., and Temple, C. (1982). *Understanding reading problems: Assessment and instruction.* Toronto, ON: Little, Brown & Co.

Henderson, E. H., and S. Templeton. (1986). A developmental perspective of formal spelling instruction through alphabet, pattern, and meaning. *Elementary School Journal,* 86(3): 304–16.

Read, Charles. (1986). *Children's Creative Spelling.* London: Routledge and Kegan Paul.

Templeton, S. (1983). Using the spelling/meaning connection to develop word knowledge in older students. *Journal of Reading*, 2(1), 8–14.

———. (1986). Synthesis of research on the learning and teaching of spelling. *Educational Leadership*, 43(6), 73–78.

———. (1991). *Teaching the integrated language arts*. Burlington, MA: Houghton Mifflin Co.

———. (1992). New trends in an historical perspective: Old story, new resolution–sound and meaning in spelling. *Language Arts*, 69(6), 454–63.

Templeton, S., and Bear, D.R. (1992). *Development of orthographic knowledge and the foundations of literacy: A memorial Festschrift for Edmund H. Henderson*. Hillsdale, NJ: Erlbaum.

# Recommended Reading List

Angeletti, S., and Peterson, R. (1993). Developing real-world spelling skills. *Learning*, 2(7), 34–36.

Azar, B. (2000). *Understanding and using English grammar.* Toronto, ON: Pearson Canada.

Bear, D. R., and Templeton, S. (1998). Explorations in developmental spelling foundations for learning and teaching phonics, spelling, and vocabulary. *Reading Teacher*, 52(3), 222–42.

Bear, Donald R., Invernizzi, M., Templeton, S., and Johnston, F. (2000). *Words their way.* Columbus, OH: Merrill/Prentice Hall.

Baghban, M. (1989). *You can help your child with writing.* Newark, DE: International Reading Association.

Bailey, K.S. (1990). *Tune in and talk.* Columbus, IN: Paper presented at the Chapter 1 Region 6 Conference, 8 May 1990.

Barber, C. (1976). *Early modern English.* Chatham, England: Andre' Deutsch Ltd.

Barron, M. (1990). *I learn to read and write the way I learn to talk: A very first book about Whole Language.* Katonah, NY: Richard C. Owen Publishers.

Bartch, J. (1992). An alternative to spelling: an integrated approach. *Language Arts*, 6(6), 404–8.

Beers, J. W. and C. S. Beers. (1977). *The logic behind children's spelling.* Cited in Booth, D., ed. (1991). *Spelling links: Reflections on spelling and its place in the curriculum.* Markham, ON: Pembroke Publishers.

Birsh, Judith R. (2005). *Multisensory teaching of basic language skills.* Baltimore, MD: Paul H. Books Publishing.

Block, K., and Peskowitz, N. (1990). Metacognition in spelling: Using writing and reading to self check spellings. *The Elementary School Journal*, 9(2), 151–64.

Bloodgood, J. (1991). A new approach to spelling instruction in language arts programs. *Elementary School Journal*, 92(2), 203–11.

Bloomfield, M.W., and Newmark, L. (1964). *A linguistic introduction to the history of English*. Toronto, ON: Random House of Canada.

Boegehold, B.D. (1984). *Getting ready to read*. Toronto, ON: Random House of Canada.

Bolton, F., and Snowball, D. (1993). *Teaching spelling: A practical resource*. Melborne, Victoria: Thomas Nelson Australia.

Bratton, E. (1992). *Ready, set, read, final report*. Harrisburg, PA: Pennsylvania State Department of Education.

Braun, C., and Thomas, V. (1983). *Learning to spell*. Toronto, ON: Gage Publishing Ltd.

Bryson, B. (1990). *The mother tongue: English and how it got that way*. New York: William Morrow and Co.

Butler, D., and Clay, M. (1987). *Reading begins at home: Preparing children for reading before they go to school*. Portsmouth, NH: Heinemann Educational Books.

Caver, C. M. (1991). *A history of English in its own words*. New York: Harper Collins.

Children's Literacy Initiative. (1992). *Creating a classroom literacy environment: A guide for teachers of preschool through second grade*. Philadelphia, PA: Children's Literacy Initiative.

Choate, J. S., ed. (1993). *Successful mainstreaming: Proven ways to detect and correct special needs*. Needham Heights, MA: Allyn and Bacon.

Claiborne, R. (1983). *Our marvelous native tongue*. Toronto, ON: Fitzhenry and Whiteside.

Clay, M. (1987). *Writing begins at home: Preparing children for writing before they go to school*. Portsmouth, NH: Heinemann Publishers.

Cochrane, O., ed. (1992). *Questions and answers about whole language*. Katonah, NY: Richard C. Owen Publishers.

Cochrane, R. (1993). *The way we word*. Saskatoon, SA: Fifth House Publishers.

Cohn, Joanne (1988). *Tutoring your child*. Sacramento, CA: California State Department of Education Collaborative.

Cooper, Pat (1993). *When stories come to school: Telling, writing, and performing stories in the early childhood classroom*. New York: Teachers and Writers.

Cross, R. (1986). Don't let soles go to waist. *The Clearing House*, 59(9), 385–86.

Cullinan, Bernice, and Bagert, Brod. (1993). *Helping children learn to read (with activities for children from infancy through age 10)*. Washington, DC: Office of Educational Research and Improvement.

Dailey, K.A. (1991). Writing in kindergarten. *Childhood Education*, 67(3), 170–75.

Davis, Beatrice G. (1991). *On the road to reading: 101 creative activities for beginning readers.* Roslyn, NY: Berrent Publications.

Doake, D. (1981). An overview of suggestions to be made for those parents who want to help their children learn to read. *Reading Manitoba,* 1(3), 11–14.

Edelsky, C., ed. (1992). *Language Arts topics and educational issues: Information sheets.* Tucson, AZ: Center for the Expansion of Language and Thinking (CELT).

Fields, M. V. (1988). Talking and writing: explaining the whole language approach to parents. *The Reading Teacher,* 4(9), 898–903.

Forester, A. D., and Reinhard, M. (1991). *On the move.* Winnipeg, MA: Peguis Publishers.

Ganschow, L. (1983). Teaching strategies for spelling success. *Academic Therapy,* 19(2), 185–93.

Gentry, J. R. (1981). Learning to spell developmentally. *The Reading Teacher,* 34(4), 378–81.

———. (1982). An analysis of developmental spelling in GYNS at WRK. *The Reading Teacher,* 36(1), 192–200.

———. (1985). You can analyze developmental spelling—and here's how to do it! *Early Years K–8,* 15(9), 44–45.

———. (2000). A retrospective on inventive spelling and a look forward. *The Reading Teacher,* 54(3), 318–32.

———. (2007). *Breakthrough in reading and writing.* New York: Scholastic.

Gentry, J. R., and Gillet, J. W. (1993). *Teaching kids to spell.* Portsmouth, NH: Heinemann Publishers.

Gill, J. T. (1992). Focus on research: Development of word knowledge as it relates to reading, spelling, and instruction. *Language Arts,* 69(6), 444–53.

Graham, S. and Voth, V. (1990). Spelling instruction, making modifications for students with learning disabilities. *Academic Therapy,* 2(4), 447–57.

Graves, D. (1983). *Writing: Teachers and children at work.* Portsmouth, NH: Heinemann.

Griffith, Priscilla L., and Leavell, J. A. (1995). There isn't much to say about spelling . . . or is there? *Childhood Education,* 72.

Guza, D. S. (1987). A comparison of daily and weekly testing on student spelling performance. *Journal of Educational Research,* 80(6), 373–76.

Hackwell, W. J. (1987). *Signs, letters, words archaeology discovers writing.* New York, NY: Macmillan.

Hansen, J. (1987). *When writers read.* Portsmouth, NH: Heinemann Publishers.

Hayes, L. F. (1990). From scribbling to writing: Smoothing the way. *Young Children,* 45(3), 62–69.

Henderson, E. H. (1990). *Teaching spelling.* Boston, MA: Houghton Mifflin Co.

Henderson, E.H., and Beers, J.W. (1980). *Developmental and cognitive aspects of learning to spell: A reflection of word knowledge.* Newark, DE: International Reading Association.

Hill, Mary W. (1989). *Home, where reading and writing begin.* Richmond Hill, ON: Scholastic–TAB Publications.

Hiroshige Nulman, J. A., and Gerber, M. M. (1984). improving spelling performance by imitating a child's errors. *Journal of Learning Disabilities,* 17(6), 328–34.

Hodges, R. E. (1981). *Learning to spell.* Urbana, IL: ERC Clearing House on Reading and Communication Skills and ECTE.

———. (1982). *Improving spelling and vocabulary in the secondary school.* Urbana, IL: ERC Clearing House on Reading and Communication Skills.

———. (1991). Smart spelling. *Instructor,* 50(7), 69–70.

James, M. (1986). Self–selected spelling. *Academic Therapy,* 21(5), 557–63.

Jenkins, R., ed. (1986). *Spelling is forever.* Carlton South, Victoria: Australian Reading Association.

Jespersen, O. (1983). *Growth and structure of the English language.* Oxford, England: Basil Blackwell Publisher.

Jongsma, K. S. (1990). Questions and answers reading–spelling links. *The Reading Teacher,* 43(8), 608–10.

Kamii, C., ed. (1991). *Early literacy: A constructivist foundation for whole language.* Washington, DC: National Education Association.

Karch, Barbara (1990). A whole language approach for kindergarten. *Gifted Child Today,* 13(6), 56–59.

Kropp, Paul (1993). *The reading solution: Making your child a reader for life.* Toronto, ON: Random House of Canada.

Lacey, Cheryl (1994). *Moving on in spelling: Strategies and activities for the whole language classroom.* Toronto, ON: Scholastic.

Laird, C. (1981). *The word: A fresh and engaging look at how words enter and leave our language.* New York: Simon and Schuster.

Lehr, F. (1986). Invented spelling and language development. *The Reading Teacher,* 39(5), 452–54.

Leith, D. (1983). *A social history of English.* London: Routledge and Kegan Paul.

MacKinnon, L. (1989). *What kind of spelling is this?* An unpublished paper written for the Calgary Board of Education Parent Teacher Conferences, 81–85. Calgary, Alberta, Canada, 1989.

Marino, J. L. (1980). What makes a good speller? *Language Arts,* 57(2), 173–176.

———. (1981). Spelling errors: From analysis to instruction. *Language Arts,* 58(5), 567–72.

Mason, J. M., ed. (1989). *Reading and writing connections.* Needham Heights, MA: Allyn and Bacon.

Matz, Karl, A. (1993). Teaching reading. *The Reading Teacher*, 47(1), 70–72

McConnell, R. E. (1979). *Our own voice*. Toronto, ON: Gage Educational Publishing Co.

McCrum, R., Cran, W., and MacNeil, R. (1991). *The story of English*. London: Faber and Faber.

McMackin, Mary, C. (1993). The parent's role in literacy development: Fostering reading strategies at home. *Childhood Education*, 69(3), 142–45.

Morris, Thea, R. (1994). *Making spelling fun*. Calgary, AB: Jelly Bean Connections.

Nagy, W.E., Herman, P. A., and Anderson, R. C. (1985). Learning words from context. *Reading Research Quarterly*, 20(2), 233–52.

Newkirk, T., and Atwell, N., eds. (1988). *Understanding writing: Ways of observing, learning, and teaching*. Portsmouth, NH: Heinemann Educational Books.

Novelli, J. (1993). Strategies for spelling success. *Instructor*, 102(9), 40–42.

O'Flahavan, J. F., and Blassberg, R. (1992). Toward an embedded model of spelling instruction for emergent literates. *Language Arts*, 69(6), 409–17.

Pei, M. (1967). *The story of the English language*. New York: J. B. Lippincott Co.

Phenix, J. (2001). *The spelling teacher's handbook*. Markham, ON: Pembroke Publishers.

Phenix, J., and Scott-Dunne, D. (1991). *Spelling instruction that makes sense*. Markham, ON: Pembroke Publishers.

———. (1994). *Spelling for parents*. Markham, ON: Pembroke Publishers.

Raines, S. C., and Canady, R. J. (1990). *The whole language kindergarten*. New York: The Teachers College Press.

Rasinski, Timothy V. (1990). *Home literacy of parents whose children are enrolled in a whole language kindergarten*. Nashville, TN: Annual Meeting of the College Reading Association.

Read, C. (1975). *Children's categorization of speech sounds in English*. Urbana, IL: National Council of Teachers of English.

Rich, S. J. (1985). The writing suitcase. *Young Children*, 40(5), 42–44.

Richards, J. C., and Gipe, J. P. (1993). Spelling lessons for gifted language arts students. *Teaching Exceptional Children*, 25(2), 12–15.

Richmond, J., and Savva, H. (1983). *Investigating our language*. London: Edward Arnold Publishers.

Routman, R. (1993). The uses and abuses of invented spelling. *Instructor*, 102(9), 36–39.

Schickedanz, J.A. (1986). *More than the ABC's: The early stages of reading*. Washington, DC: The National Association for the Education of Young Children.

———. (1990). *Adam's righting revolutions*. Portsmouth, NH: Heinemann Educational Book.

Schlagal, R. C., and Schlagal, J. H. (1992). The integral character of spelling: teaching strategies for multiple purposes. *Language Arts*, 69(6), 418–24.

Scott, R., and Siamon, S. (1994). *Sharing the secrets teach your child to spell.* Toronto, ON: Macmillan Canada.

Shaw, H. (1993). *Spell it right!* New York: Harper Collins Publishers.

Smith, Frank. (1982). *Writing and the writer.* New York: Holt Rinehart and Winston.

Staab, Claire, F. (1990). Teacher mediation in one whole literacy classroom. *The Reading Teacher*, 43, 548–52.

Strickland, D. S., and Morrow, L. M. (1989). Emerging readers and writers: Young children's early writing development. *The Reading Teacher*, 42(6), 426–27.

———, eds. (1989). *Emerging literacy: Young children learn to read and write.* Newark, DE: International Reading Association.

Tarasoff, M. (1990). *Spelling strategies you can teach.* Victoria, BC: Pixelart Graphics.

———. (1992). *A guide to children's spelling development for parents and teachers.* Victoria BC: Active Learning Institute.

Templeton, S. (1983). Using the spelling/meaning connection to develop word knowledge in older students. *Journal of Reading*, 2(1), 8–14.

———. (1986). Synthesis of research on the learning and teaching of spelling. *Educational Leadership*, 43(6), 73–78.

———. (1991). *Teaching the integrated language arts.* Burlington, MA: Houghton Mifflin Co.

———. (1992). New trends in an historical perspective: Old story, new resolution–sound and meaning in spelling. *Language Arts*, 69(6), 454–63.

Templeton, S., and Bear, D. R. (1992). *Development of orthographic knowledge and the foundations of literacy: A memorial Festschrift for Edmund H. Henderson.* Hillsdale, NJ: Erlbaum.

Texas Education Agency. (1991). *Spelling instruction: A proper perspective.* Austin, TX: Publications Distribution Office, Texas Education Agency.

Thompson, M., and Block, K. (1990). Practice format, length of training, and spelling test performance of fifth and sixth graders. *Elementary School Journal*, 91(1), 77–87.

Throne, J. (1988). Becoming a kindergarten of readers. *Young Children*, 43(6), 10–17.

Tompkins, G. E., and Yarden, D. B. (1986). *Answering students' questions about words.* Urbana, IL: ERIC Clearing House on Reading and Communication Skills and NCTE.

Weaver, C. (1982). Welcoming errors as signs of growth. *Language Arts*, 59(5), 438–44.

Wilde, S. (1992). *You kan red this!: Spelling and punctuation for whole language classrooms, K–6*. Portsmouth, NH: Heinemann Publishing.

Yatvin, J. (1979). How to get good spelling from poor spellers. *Learning*, 8(1), 122–28.

# About The Author

**Roberta Heembrock** earned her elementary education degree from Acadia University in Wolfville, Nova Scotia. For fourteen years, she taught regular education and special education, including the gifted and talented. Roberta has written and presented curriculum at the school, board, and national levels, mainly in language arts and mathematics.

Roberta lives in Calgary, Alberta, with her husband, Peter, her two daughters, Sara and Natalie, and her pet dog, Noodles. This is her first book.